THE
POWER OF
DIVINE
BREATH

Sheik Dr. Ismail Bin HJ Kassim

PARTRIDGE

To order additional copies of this book, contact
Toll Free 800 101 2657 (Singapore)
Toll Free 1 800 81 7340 (Malaysia)
orders.singapore@partridgepublishing.com

www.partridgepublishing.com/singapore

Contents

Preface vii

Introduction...ix

Foreword From Perahmat Head Of Units...............xiii

Glossary xxiii

From: North Malaysia 1

From: Central Malaysia......................................22

From: South Malaysia 96

From: Singapore 102

From: East Malaysia 108

From: Aceh, Indonesia....................................... 115

From: Pakistan 125

بِسْمِ اللهِ الرَّحْمَنِ الرَّحِيمِ

اَللّٰهُمَّ صَلِّ عَلَى سَيِّدِنَا مُحَمَّدٍ وَعَلَى اٰلِ سَيِّدِنَا مُحَمَّدٍ

Preface

In the name of ALLAH سبحانه و تعالى, the most gracious and the most merciful. Praises only for ALLAH سبحانه و تعالى and blessings and peace be upon our prophet Muhammad صلى الله عليه وسلم.

Through the openings of the knowledge of لا إِلَهَ إِلَّا اللَّه and blessing from our master Sultanul Awliya Sheikh Abdul Qadir Al Jilani and the golden chain of awliyas until our master in this time Mursyidul Muqmineen Sultanul Ariffin Syed Noorullah Shah Arifudeen Al Jilani, the secrets of zikrul anfas has been passed down the generations since the time of our Prophet Muhammad صلى الله عليه وسلم.

This book of testimonies is about the sharing of experiences of those people who has learned about zikrul anfas. They will share about the peace, tranquility and secrets that they have found with zikrul anfas. This is a book of testimonies proving that peace of mind and heart are truly achievable and can be learned from the master who has this knowledge.

Special thanks to brother Azman, Haris, Badrul, Tengku Bahaudeen, Rashidan, Shamsul, Saharudin and sister Sharifah Nor, Zarina, Arlizah, Nor Azian who made this book a reality with their sincere contributions of funds. Alhamdulillah.

Special thanks to brother Saharudin, Rashidan, Iskandar, Shaharel and sister Nor Azian, Syafiza, Syarifah Farhana, Mariam Abdul Razak who help to edit and translate the manuscript, provided photographs, CD covers, posters and made publishing this book possible. Alhamdulillah.

SHEIKH DR ISMAIL BIN HJ KASSIM – RAHMATAN LIL'ALAMIN ORGANIZATION

Dargah Sharif. Ajmer, India – Group Salawat
And Qasidah During The Night

Introduction

What is zikrul anfas? Zikrul Anfas is defined as the breath that is in remembrance of ALLAH سبحانه و تعالى سبحانه و تعالى. The breath that is in remembrance of ALLAH سبحانه و تعالى سبحانه و تعالى, will always be at peace as love and blessings are constantly showered to the person who is in zikrul anfas state.

Referring to the surah Al Fath verse 10. A covenant and promise made to ALLAH سبحانه و تعالى سبحانه و تعالى, will be rewarded with zikrul anfas.

Majority of the people with zikrul anfas, will always be positive minded and patient. They will not be troubled by anything and seldom have problems hitting them. This is because they are continuously in remembrance of ALLAH سبحانه و تعالى سبحانه و تعالى 24 hours of the time. Hence, blessings upon blessings, peace upon peace are given to them from ALLAH سبحانه و تعالى سبحانه و تعالى.

There is a vast ocean of knowledge about zikrul anfas that culminates from the knowledge of لَا إِلَهَ إِلَّا اللَّه, the confession of unity. There is a need to have a Mursyid or master to teach and guide the person on zikrul anfas and لَا إِلَهَ إِلَّا اللَّه. There are many benefits of zikrul anfas. Some of the benefits are such as i) peace and tranquility with every breath, ii) strong and positive mindset, iii) removes stress, iv) sharp mind and thought process.

In Malaysia, we are blessed to have Al Faqir IllALLAH سبحانه و تعالى Sheikh Dr Ismail Kassim who is teaching this knowledge. Sheikh Dr Ismail Kassim has studied this knowledge for more than 25 years from his master, Mursyidul Muqmineen Sultanul Ariffin Syed Noorullah Shah Arifudeen Al Jilani.

Sheikh Dr Ismail Kassim is also the founder, advisor, main speaker and mursyid to Rahmatan Lil ' Alamin Organization jamaah in Malaysia, Brunei, Indonesia, India, Pakistan, China and Middle East countries. He is recognized and supported by Ahli Sunnah Wal Jamaah Ulamas all over the world for his tireless dakwah work. He is the recipient of Nelson Mandela Award 2014, Malaysia's Tokoh Perpaduan Negara 2015, Awards from Open University and Universities from India, England and America.

Rahmatan Lil 'Alamin Organization, under the stewardship of Sheikh Dr Ismail Kassim consists of sub functional units to drive the dakwah work in an effective and efficient manner. The sub functional units are PERAHMAT, RAHMANITA, YAGEM, YOURAH, MADRASAH DARUL ULUM, PERAHMAT MEDIA BROADCAST, PERAHMAT PUBLISHER, PERAHMAT EVENT MANAGEMENT, PERAHMAT QURBAN SERVICES AND DAKWAH UNIT.

Sheikh Dr Ismail Kassim has been at the forefront of promoting peace and tranquility of body and mind through the teaching of zikrul anfas and the knowledge of لَا إِلَهَ إِلَّا اللَّه. Zikrul Anfas is the technique of getting the breath to move in tandem with the soul and achieving positive and peaceful mind. Through the knowledge of لَا إِلَهَ إِلَّا اللَّه, the power of zikrul anfas can be harness beyond our physical and spiritual limit to open the human mind and heart to the highest spiritual experience.

In this book of testimony, you will see CDs, posters, banners and photographs of the places where Sheikh Dr Ismail Kassim and Rahmatan Lil'Alamin Organization jamaah have travelled in their quest to spread and share the knowledge from the first pillar of Islam. Syahadah, the knowledge of لَا إِلَهَ إِلَّا اللَّهُ مُحَمَّدٌ رَسُوْلُ اللَّهِ, the confession of unity.

View Of Ajmer Of Township

Ajmer Business And Shopping Area

Foreword From Perahmat Head Of Units

Dr. Yahya Muhamad,
Vice President
Rahmatan Lil Alameen Organization (PERAHMAT)

Before learning the knowledge of Kalimah لا إله إلا الله, as a prerequisite to follow ALLAH سبحانه و تعالى's commandment "فَاعْلَمْ أَنَّهُ لَا إِلَهَ إِلَّا اللَّهُ" (Al-Quran, 47:19), I acknowledge that a muslim will not know his **ILAH** and by not knowing his **ILAH**, he will not have faith and believe in ALLAH سبحانه و تعالى سبحانه و تعالى. By understanding the knowledge of Kalimah, we will also realize that the knowledge brings a person to "Syahadah". The knowledge of Syahadah is the core to understanding and practicing the First Pillar of Islam. With a perfect Syahadah, a person's zikrul anfas will come alive and connects to ALLAH سبحانه و تعالى Rabbul Alamin.

Hj Shamsul Kahar,
Head of Dakwah Unit
PERAHMAT

Alhamdulillah, all praises to **ALLAH** سبحانه و تعالى .سبحانه و تعالى

Syukur, to ALLAH سبحانه و تعالى All Mighty for his blessings and grace that is showered upon us every second of the time and with every breath that we take. Not a second pass without ALLAH سبحانه و تعالى's purview. Peace and blessings upon our beloved **Prophet Muhammad** صلى الله عليه وسلم

"We did not send you (O ' Muhammad), but as a mercy to the alamin(mankind, jinns and all that

exist)". (Al-Anbiyaa' 21:107) ALLAH سبحانه و تعالى umma salli ala Sayyidina Muhammad wa ala alihi wa sahbihi wasalam ﷺ.

Alhamdulillah, eversince we received zikrul anfas and we started learning about the knowledge of لا إله إلا الله, we realize that our understanding and knowledge of the kalimah is limited and strayed. Before learning this knowledge from a true Mursyid, our understanding was based from our own ideology and narrow mind set. Without learning the knowledge of لا إله إلا الله which is the highest knowledge that ALLAH سبحانه و تعالى has bestowed upon mankind, we will all be lost. There is a need to find a mursyid who carries the knowledge of ALLAH سبحانه و تعالى سبحانه و تعالى. Find him and learn from him. When you have found the carrier of the knowledge, you will also find the rope that connects you to ALLAH سبحانه و تعالى سبحانه و تعالى and that is the zikrul anfas. Where every breath is zikr and remembrance to ALLAH سبحانه و تعالى All Mighty.

Zainul Anuar bin Abdullah,

Head of Perahmat Event Management &
Perahmat Media Broadcast (PEM & PMB)

Alhamdulillah, I'm so grateful to ALLAH سبحانه و تعالى All Mighty for his blessings and love that, I and my family has been chosen to learn the highest knowledge of لا إله إلا الله and gifted with zikrul anfas. The knowledge of لا إله إلا الله has been passed down the generations of Prophet Muhammad's ﷺ Ahlul Bayt through centuries up until now in the modern era. Our family is priviledge to have a mursyid who is from the lineage of Prophet Muhammad teaching us the knowledge of لا إله إلا الله and the secrets of zikrul anfas.

Peace and blessings to our beloved Prophet Muhammad ﷺ and to all our masyaikh, who have tirelessly taught this highest knowledge to us all so that we understand and know our **ILAH**, **ROBB** & **ALLAH** سبحانه و تعالى سبحانه و تعالى.

Mohd Razali B Mohd Salleh
Head of Perahmat Publisher

Verily, **ALLAH** سبحانه و تعالى سبحانه و تعالى and the Angels gives salawat to Prophet **Muhammad** ﷺ. Oh, all my mukmin brothers and sisters, please give salawat and salam to our Prophet Muhammad ﷺ.

Alhamdulillah. Syukur to ALLAH سبحانه و تعالى who gives us the connection of zikrul anfas and a mursyid who teaches us with all sincerity and patience and he is also our witness in front of ALLAH سبحانه و تعالى All Mighty.

Before I learned about the knowledge of لا إله إلا الله (First pillar of islam), I truly believed that ALLAH سبحانه و تعالى exist with all his omnipotent powers. Still, I felt that **ALLAH** سبحانه و تعالى سبحانه و تعالى is so far away, too far, yet ALLAH سبحانه و تعالى سبحانه و تعالى says that he is near to his servants, very near. And I didn't feel the love for **Rasulullah** ﷺ, only that I know, **Rasullullah** ﷺ is my prophet.

However, after receiving the baiat of zikrul anfas and learning the knowledge of لا إله إلا الله, I changed and with zikrul anfas, I felt the connection to ALLAH سبحانه و تعالى سبحانه و تعالى and Rasulullah ﷺ all the time. Gradually I became more at peace and able to differentiate between **HAQ** and **BATHIL**.

Dr Khadijah binti Md Jadi,
President of RahmaNita
(Women Development)

السلام عليكم ورحمة الله وبركاته
الحمد لله ربّ العالمين

All praises to ALLAH سبحانه و تعالى سبحانه و تعالى, the All Mighty. I am forever grateful to ALLAH سبحانه و تعالى سبحانه و تعالى for giving me a mursyid who gave me the connection to ALLAH سبحانه و تعالى through zikrul anfas and introduced to me the knowledge of لا إله إلا الله that made me understand about **ILAH** dan **ROBB.** The first pillar of islam, which is the knowledge of syahadah made understanding the knowledge of لا

إله إلا الله easier to learn and made me understand the following:

1. Understand what is **ILAH** and **ROBB.**
2. Know that we are weak and helpless.
3. A method to remove shirk from your heart and soul.
4. Removes arrogant attitude and ego from self.
5. Achieve peace and tranquility.
6. Very easy to remember **ALLAH** سبحانه و تعالى سبحانه و تعالى in your heart and soul and my target is to remember **ALLAH** سبحانه تعالى سبحانه و تعالى و 24 hours.
7. Enjoy the pleasure of zikrullah and iman.
8. Very focused and peace of mind.

Zarina Anwar Layani
Secretary Yayasan Gerakan
Ekonomi Mukmin

Alhamdullillah and Syukur to **ALLAH** سبحانه و تعالى سبحانه و تعالى who gifted us with zikrul anfas, that gives connection to ALLAH 24 سبحانه و تعالى hours of the time. ALLAH سبحانه و تعالى سبحانه و تعالى then gives us the the knowledge of Kalimah لا إله إلا الله, the highest knowledge from the first pillar of islam.

I've now reached my 2nd year in learning this knowledge and I feel my transformation, where previously, I only know the word **ALLAH** سبحانه و تعالى سبحانه و تعالى and **Rasulullah** ﷺ. And utterance of kalimah **ALLAH** سبحانه و تعالى سبحانه و تعالى, only from the lips but never penetrate the heart. I was truly ignorant and I felt, all this time, I was cheating ALLAH و سبحانه تعالى سبحانه و تعالى.

Now, with zikrul anfas we are always connected to ALLAH سبحانه و تعالى سبحانه و تعالى and we are always at peace. And learning the knowledge of kalimah from Mursyid Sheikh Dr Ismail Kassim, our zikrul anfas becomes stronger as we are filled with the knowledge of لا إله إلا الله. Eventhough, we are slowly learning, yet we feel our life changing from darkness to light with the guidance from ALLAH سبحانه و تعالى سبحانه و تعالى.

Mohd Nor Majnon
Head of Perahmat Sales & Marketing

For 40 years, I did not know there was a knowledge of لا إله إلا الله from the first pillar of islam, the practice of syahadah and the remembrance of ALLAH سبحانه و تعالى سبحانه و تعالى 24 hours of the time through zikrul anfas.

Alhamdu lillah. After meeting Mursyid Sheikh Dr Ismail who taught the knowledge of لا إله إلا الله and after practicing it in my daily life, I started to feel a huge change in myself. Where I am always at peace in all types of situation that I'm faced with good or bad. With zikrul anfas, I'm always in remembrance of ALLAH و سبحانه تعالى and all negative aspect in life could not affect me especially when I'm in the state of zikrul anfas.

Previously, my prayers was very physical, meaningless and following others. Now, after learning the knowledge of لا إله إلا الله I feel the sweetness in doing my prayers. The pleasure in ablution, pleasure in jamaah prayers. Ya **ALLAH** سبحانه و تعالى, only **ALLAH** سبحانه و تعالى سبحانه و تعالى knows the pleasure attained through the kalimah of لا إله إلا الله.

YOUTH
PERAHMAT

Hadi Iskandar
President Youth of Perahmat (YouRah)

Alhamdulillah, we are very fortunate at our young age for the gift of zikrul anfas from ALLAH سبحانه و تعالى All Mighty. With zikrul anfas we are connected to ALLAH سبحانه و تعالى سبحانه و تعالى and Rasullullah 24 ﷺ hours of the time. The connection opens up our heart and with the teaching from mursyid Sheikh Dr Ismail Kassim on the knowledge of kalimah لا إله إلا الله which is the knowledge brought down through the lineage of prophet Muhammad ﷺ by his progeny Ahlul Bayt since 1436 years ago.

We are the Youth of Perahmat who carries the responsibility of ensuring the knowledge and the culture brought down by our prophet Muhammad continues it's legacy to the future. May ALLAH سبحانه و تعالى سبحانه و تعالى bless all of us, who is in this path carrying the flag of لا إله إلا الله to continue spreading the knowledge of syahadah and لا إله إلا الله to all our brothers and sisters out there. May ALLAH سبحانه و تعالى سبحانه و تعالى save the ummah of prophet Muhammad ﷺ, may ALLAH سبحانه و تعالى سبحانه و تعالى forgive the ummah of prophet Muhammad ﷺ. Ameen.

Glossary

YAGEM : Yayasan Gerakan Ekonomi Mukmin

YOURAH : Youth of Perahmat

MBP : Majlis Belia Perahmat

RAHMANITA : Perahmat Women Wing

UNIT DAKWAH : Missionary Unit

PERAHMAT: Rahmatan Lil'Alamin Organization

MDU : Madrasah Darul Ulum

PP : Perahmat Publisher

PEM : Perahmat Event Management

Zikr : Rememberance

Zikrul Anfas / Zikr Anfas : Remembrance of the Breath.

Bai'at : The act of solemn pledge; binding pledge; covenant

Haq : Right, Correct

Batil : Wrong

Mursyid : Spiritual Teacher

Syukur : Thankful

Mazmumah : Wrongdoing

Syirik : Shirk

Nafs : Inner Self

From: North Malaysia

Name: Che Salmah Binti Mehamood
Age: 62 Years
From: Bandar Baru Bangi, Selangor.

بِسْمِ اللهِ الرَّحْمٰنِ الرَّحِيْمِ
اللَّهُمَّ صَلِّ عَلَى مُحَمَّدٍ وَعَلَى آلِ مُحَمَّدٍ
فَاعْلَمْ أَنَّهُ لَا إِلَهَ إِلَّا اللَّهُ
وتالله وبالله والله

Testimonials: Alhamdu Lillah, Thankfully, I was bai'at
and talkin with the zikr of the breath by Tuan Guru

1

Qutbul Mashaikh Mufti Syed Noori Arifudheen Jilani Sarkar Qibla at his residence in Hyderabad with a few others on Jumaat of February 2013. It was an amazing experience when getting bai'at. While holding the fabric that connects us with the teacher felt like there is a flow of electricity. This situation is felt until the completion of the ritual. After the talkin by wife of Sarkar with سبحانه و تعالى HU ALLAH سبحانه و تعالى ALLAH and after I practiced a few times, I felt that I can already breathe with ALLAH سبحانه و تعالى HU ALLAH سبحانه و تعالى. When I closed my eyes, practicing Zikr of the breath, SubhanALLAH سبحانه و تعالى, I always noticed two beautiful eyes looking calmly at me. It felt like someone close to me is watching over me.

Alhamdu Lillah, with consistently doing regular Zikr Anfas and attending the knowledge session about Kalimah لا إله إلا الله conducted by Tuan Sheikh Dr. Ismail Bin Hj Kassim, my Zikrul Anfas becomes stronger and my heart becomes peaceful. There is nothing to be worried about due to the fact that all under the purview and authority of ALLAH و سبحانه تعالى سبحانه و تعالى. I feel guarded, and loved by ALLAH سبحانه و تعالى سبحانه و تعالى at all times. Thus we will feel the longing and remember ALLAH سبحانه و تعالى سبحانه و تعالى by doing zikr.

When the heart is calm and breathe with ALLAH سبحانه و تعالى HU ALLAH سبحانه و تعالى, I felt my prayer to be more humble, because we will be more

The Power of Divine Breath

focused on remembering ALLAH سبحانه سبحانه و تعالى
و تعالى upon us. Perhaps even syaitan will not bother us
when we activate zikrul anfas. We also feel more
diligent, love and confident in worship and in reaching
out to others who need help. I pray my zikrul anfas will
last until I am called back to ALLAH سبحانه و تعالى
سبحانه و تعالى and that my last breath will be ALLAH
سبحانه و تعالى سبحانه و تعالى and my last word is لا إله إلا
الله.

Name: -Withheld- (Student of The University Malaysia
in Kelantan)
Age: 24 years

بِسْمِ اللهِ الرَّحْمٰنِ الرَّحِيْمِ
اللَّهُمَّ صَلِّ عَلَى مُحَمَّدٍ وَعَلَى آلِ مُحَمَّدٍ
فَاعْلَمْ أَنَّهُ لَا إِلٰهَ إِلَّا اللَّهُ
وتالله وبالله والله

Alhamdulilah, grateful to the divine grace of ALLAH
سبحانه و تعالى سبحانه و تعالى for bringing me to this path.
All this while, I've been looking for peace of soul
through the religious knowledge and sciences. After
reaching out to learn the breath zikr, I feel that I'm
being reborn and my soul feels very tranquil. My heart
is no longer like before. Previously, I always think
negatively about any issues or problems.

Now, I feel my soul and thought is so positive; so much
so, that things that used to upset me and make me

become very angry, does not stress me anymore. I was the person who will think negatively, and at times, I dare to hurt someone who hurt me. Now, I do not seem to mind with all that, I've tasted the sweetness, to forgive others and very happy with what I have. The feeling of love for Prophet Muhammad ﷺ is so deep, and the love for ALLAH سبحانه و تعالى سبحانه و تعالى have increased tremendously. Prayers for me now is so easy, without feeling heavy and no longer done solely to meet the needs as a Muslim. The feeling is now more towards wanting to worship, and be accepted by ALLAH سبحانه و تعالى سبحانه و تعالى, and wanting to be a true believer. InsyaALLAH سبحانه و تعالى, I'll continue to be in this path, until the end of my life. I am confident that this knowledge will help me in the afterlife. Amin.

POSTERS AND BANNERS OF PROGRAMS BY RAHMATAN LIL' ALAMIN ORGANIZATION

DVD'S ON TALKS AND LECTURE BY
SHEIKH DR ISMAIL KASSIM PUBLISHED BY
RAHMATAN LIL 'ALAMIN ORGANIZATION

Magnet Nafas Program In Malacca Malaysia

Name: -Withheld-
Age: -undisclosed-
From: Kedah

بِسْمِ اللهِ الرَّحْمٰنِ الرَّحِيْمِ

اللَّهُمَّ صَلِّ عَلَى مُحَمَّدٍ وَعَلَى آلِ مُحَمَّدٍ

فَاعْلَمْ أَنَّهُ لَا إِلٰهَ إِلَّا اللَّهُ

وتاللهِ وباللهِ واللهِ

Assalamualaikum warahmatullah hiwabarokatuh...
سبحانه و تعالىi, waALLAH سبحانه و تعالىi, WaALLAH
waALLAH سبحانه و تعالىi ... What I am about to tell
you is true ... The first time I saw my teacher Mursyid
Sheikh Dr Ismail Kassim and Sheikh explained the
knowledge of Kalimah لا إله إلا الله and the zikir of the
breath, propelled me to pursue the knowledge.

Before accepting the knowledge, I made istiqorah and
hajat prayers to ask for guidance from ALLAH سبحانه
و تعالى سبحانه و تعالى. Alhamdullillah, after I took bai'at
from Sheikh, I felt closer to ALLAH سبحانه و تعالى
سبحانه و تعالى and my heart and qalbu exploded with
emotion towards Rasulullah ﷺ. When Sheikh
returned to Kuala Lumpur, my mind was muddled and
confused, probably, due to lack of faith and knowledge,
added on by ongoing act of defamation – I was not so
strong.

However, I held on, remained confident in ALLAH
سبحانه و تعالى سبحانه و تعالى and kept on practicing the

Zikrul Anfas (ALLAH سبحانه و تعالى Hu ALLAH سبحانه و تعالى). My Emir, invited me to the Zikr Sessions. I am very happy with the session, my knowledge can be enhanced further, and beneficial as reminders when I forget. As days passed by, news about the arrival of Sheikh Dr Ismail Kassim to Kedah came to me which made me very happy and can't wait to meet with Sheikh Dr Ismail Kassim.

Alhamdullillah with permission and blessings of ALLAH سبحانه و تعالى سبحانه و تعالى on 31ˢᵗ January 2014, I finally met Sheikh. During the training of zikrul anfas, the feeling of yearning, missing our Prophet Muhammad ﷺ was so great, prompted me to make doa so that I could meet our beloved Prophet Muhammad ﷺ.

Next day, after the Fajr prayer, while doing zikr of لا إله إلا الله, I saw, before my eyes, the word "محمد"in the shadows. SubhanALLAH إسبحانه و تعالى My tears flowed and I said "Oh ALLAH سبحانه و تعالى, Peace Be Upon My Prophet ?". When I performed my prayers, I felt happy and remembered our great Prophet Muhammad ﷺ and tears flowed again. Oh ALLAH سبحانه و تعالى سبحانه و Only ALLAH سبحانه و تعالى تعالى knows my feeling at the time. There are a lot of experience where I felt the presence of 'nur' in my heart which I cannot describe because only ALLAH و سبحانه تعالى سبحانه و تعالى knows what's in my heart. Oh ALLAH سبحانه و تعالى سبحانه و تعالى, Allow me to meet our beloved Prophet Muhammad ﷺ

Name: -Withheld- (Lecturer)
Age: 28 Years
From: Gerik, Perak

بِسْمِ اللهِ الرَّحْمٰنِ الرَّحِيْمِ
اللَّهُمَّ صَلِّ عَلَى مُحَمَّدٍ وَعَلَى آلِ مُحَمَّدٍ
فَاعْلَمْ أَنَّهُ لَا إِلٰهَ إِلَّا اللَّهُ
وتالله وبالله والله

I'm blessed to have found the path that I have been searching for, all these years. Since taking bai'at of zikir of the breath or Zikrul Anfas, I now feel:

1. Peace beyond imagination.
2. Easy to perform the prayer with sincerity
3. Every task become easy.
4. Providence and needs are always never in doubt.
5. Deep feeling of love and affection for Rasulullah ﷺ
6. Strong belief in ALLAH سبحانه و تعالى سبحانه و تعالى and the Messenger.
7. The sweetness of doing prayers.
8. The sweetness to forgive others.
9. True happiness.
10. Envy towards friends who have long passed away.
11. Chasing eternal life in akhirah or Afterlife.

Name: -Withheld- (Self Employed)

Age: 26 Years

From: Gerik, Perak.

بِسْمِ اللهِ الرَّحْمٰنِ الرَّحِيْمِ

اللَّهُمَّ صَلِّ عَلَى مُحَمَّدٍ وَعَلَى آلِ مُحَمَّدٍ

فَاعْلَمْ أَنَّهُ لَا إِلٰهَ إِلَّا اللَّهُ

وتالله وبالله والله

Alhamdulilah. Thanks to ALLAH سبحانه و تعالى سبحانه و تعالى I feel peace when doing my prayers, and my family life is much happier than ever. It is now easier to carry out duties in my daily life including prayers. With zikr of the breath, I'm able to earn a living like a responsible Muslim. I also know of the need, to be a true believer and not just a normal Muslim. Previously, I used to pray just to fulfill my duties as a Muslim. But now, I perform my prayers sincerely for the love of ALLAH سبحانه و تعالى AlMighty and for Rasulullah صلى الله عليه وسلم. And now, with the zikrul anfas, I feel happy, peaceful and always remember ALLAH سبحانه و تعالى سبحانه و تعالى for his bounty of grace to us and I'm no more stressed thinking of the worldly affairs. Everything can be dealt with easily. Trials and tribulation in this life can be accepted with an open mind. I am confident that with this knowledge, I'm able to change, to become a true Muslim believer and I hope learn more about ALLAH سبحانه و تعالى سبحانه و تعالى and his vast knowledge. Indeed ALLAH سبحانه و تعالى is most rich, wise and gracious. As his humble servant, we need to find the knowledge already clearly stated in the Quraan. I'm blessed to have found this righteous path. I hope to be in this path till the Judgment day where all man and woman will be gathered.

Name: -Withheld- (Polytechnic Student of Tuanku Sultanah Bahiyah)
Age: -undisclosed-
From: Kedah

بِسْمِ اللهِ الرَّحْمٰنِ الرَّحِيْم

اللَّهُمَّ صَلِّ عَلَى مُحَمَّدٍ وَعَلَى آلِ مُحَمَّدٍ

فَاعْلَمْ أَنَّهُ لَا إِلٰهَ إِلَّا اللّٰهُ

وتالله وبالله والله

Assalamualaikum.

Long before I got bai'at of zikrul anfas, I was not a confident person. At that time I thought if I had deviated from the true path, I wondered what would have happened to me. As my heart beats strongly, Satan whispered to me not to be confident, but I was only the creation of ALLAH سبحانه و تعالى سبحانه و تعالى and I needed to submit all of me in spirit, body and nafs, to ALLAH سبحانه و تعالى. During the time I received the Bai'at of zikrul anfas, I thought of all the sins that I have done. I felt that if ALLAH سبحانه و تعالى سبحانه و تعالى does not forgive all my sins, I am a sure-loser. At the time of bai'at, I felt Sheikh Dr Ismail Hj Kassim holding my heart and whispering Kalimah ALLAH و سبحانه

تعالى سبحانه و تعالى into my ears, I burst into tears. Then, I sensed a light in my eyes and my body felt so cold. After the bai'at, my breathing feels different from before, my eyes feel brighter than ever before.

I thank ALLAH سبحانه و تعالى سبحانه و تعالى for bringing me into this path and I feel a deep love for Rasulullah ﷺ. Nowadays, I start any conversations with friends by talking about religious knowledge and I try to avoid empty talks. I feel my spirituality, changed immediately after my bai'at. When I do wrong or bad things, my heart beats hard and my breath becomes strong and fast. I believe in Kalimah ALLAH و سبحانه تعالى سبحانه و تعالى and I will not do anything that will cause wrath of ALLAH سبحانه و تعالى سبحانه و تعالى. Amin. Not forgetting, my teachers who guide me to the path of ALLAH سبحانه و تعالى سبحانه. In the name of ALLAH سبحانه و تعالى سبحانه و تعالى, I now feel very close to Rasullullah ﷺ.

MUZAKARAH AND DISCUSSION AT
MAGNET NAFAS PROGRAM

Village Of Nurishah, Hyderabad. India

Nurishah, Hyderabad. India – Sheikh Dr
Ismail Kassim Lecturing To Jamaah

Nurishah, Hyderabad. India – Sugar cane juice making

****

Name: -Withheld- (Polytechnic Student of Tuanku Sultanah Bahiyah)
Age: -undisclosed-
From: Kedah

بِسْمِ اللهِ الرَّحْمٰنِ الرَّحِيْمِ
اللَّهُمَّ صَلِّ عَلَى مُحَمَّدٍ وَعَلَى آلِ مُحَمَّدٍ
فَاعْلَمْ أَنَّهُ لَا إِلَهَ إِلَّا اللَّهُ
وتاللّه وبـاللّه واللّه

Assalamualaikum,

The experience I went through is very valuable for myself because the experience teaches me to be closer to ALLAH سبحانه و تعالى و تعالى سبحانه and makes me realize that I'm actually a humble slave or servant of ALLAH سبحانه و تعالى سبحانه و تعالى. Before I took bai'at, a lot of thing was in my mind and there was an inner voice in me saying that I will not be able to follow all things and requirements needed to do after bai'at.

However, I put aside such feelings and I said to myself "maybe, this is the way that ALLAH سبحانه و تعالى سبحانه و تعالى has set for me and I submit everything to ALLAH سبحانه و تعالى". During the bai'at, I felt emotional when I recalled the things that I have done; yet ALLAH سبحانه و تعالى's love for his servant, have led me to this righteous path and I thank ALLAH سبحانه و تعالى سبحانه و تعالى for his grace for guiding me. When the Kalimah ALLAH سبحانه و تعالى سبحانه و تعالى was whispered to my ears during bai'at, I felt emotional but I did not cry, and my body felt cold. After the bai'at ritual completed, I finally cried. I'm so grateful to ALLAH سبحانه و تعالى سبحانه و تعالى for not only, having me on this righteous path, but also, having Sheikh Dr Ismail Kassim as my Mursyid. I do realize, that ALLAH سبحانه و تعالى سبحانه و تعالى has planned everything for his servants. Alhamdulillah, the feeling and yearning for ALLAH سبحانه و تعالى سبحانه و تعالى, to love and to be loved, is really what true love is all about.

****

Name: -Withheld- (Self Employed)

Age: 31 Years
From: Kedah

بِسْمِ اللهِ الرَّحْمٰنِ الرَّحِيْمِ
اللَّهُمَّ صَلِّ عَلَى مُحَمَّدٍ وَعَلَى آلِ مُحَمَّدٍ
فَاعْلَمْ أَنَّهُ لَا إِلٰهَ إِلَّا اللَّهُ
وتالله وبالله والله

After receiving bai'at, I have changed a lot. Previously, I was so impatient but now I'm very patient, I think about death constantly and I feel ashamed to ALLAH سبحانه و تعالى سبحانه و تعالى for all the wrong doings that I have done all this time in my life. I now feel peaceful, can accept advice and think first before making decisions. Nowadays, I hate vices and do not like to talk about other people. I thank my brother and I thank ALLAH سبحانه و تعالى سبحانه و تعالى for meeting me up with Sheikh Dr Ismail Kassim. Previously, I pretended to pray to gain fame. Now when people mentions Rasulullah's ﷺ name, I will cry. I miss Rasullullah ﷺ. Now, I feel, there's always peace in my prayers.

****

Name: -Withheld- (Trader)
Age: 58 years.
From: Kedah

بِسْمِ اللهِ الرَّحْمٰنِ الرَّحِيْمِ

اللّٰهُمَّ صَلِّ عَلٰى مُحَمَّدٍ وَعَلٰى آلِ مُحَمَّدٍ

فَاعْلَمْ أَنَّهُ لَا إِلٰهَ إِلَّا اللّٰهُ

وتالله وبالله والله

I am now very peaceful and tranquil after getting bai'at. Previously, I don't do much zikr and salawat but now I want to do it all the time. Prayers is easy to do now, compared to before.

****

Name: -Withheld- (Lecturer at Politeknik Tuanku Sultanah Bahiyah)
Age: 31 Years
From: Kedah

بِسْمِ اللهِ الرَّحْمٰنِ الرَّحِيْمِ

اللّٰهُمَّ صَلِّ عَلٰى مُحَمَّدٍ وَعَلٰى آلِ مُحَمَّدٍ

فَاعْلَمْ أَنَّهُ لَا إِلٰهَ إِلَّا اللّٰهُ

وتالله وبالله والله

Alhamdulillah ... After receiving the Zikrul anfas*, I feel love for Rasullullah ﷺ increasing. My trust in ALLAH سبحانه و تعالى becomes strong, especially if there are problems, I submit to و سبحانه

تعالى and Rasullullah ﷺ and pray for blessing. Doing prayers now, feels so easy.

****

Name: -Withheld- (Lecturer at Politeknik Tuanku Sultanah Bahiyah)
Age: 35 years
From: Kedah

بِسْمِ اللهِ الرَّحْمٰنِ الرَّحِيْمِ

اللَّهُمَّ صَلِّ عَلَى مُحَمَّدٍ وَعَلَى آلِ مُحَمَّدٍ

فَاعْلَمْ أَنَّهُ لَا إِلٰهَ إِلَّا اللَّهُ

وتالله وبالله والله

Alhamdulillah, thank ALLAH سبحانه و تعالى سبحانه و تعالى for his bounty and most valuable is the grace of faith, Islam and benevolence. In ALLAH سبحانه و تعالى, سبحانه و تعالى, I seek various ways (wusul) which would bring me to ALLAH سبحانه و تعالى سبحانه و تعالى. With the grace of Ar-Rahman and Ar-Rahim ALLAH سبحانه و تعالى سبحانه و تعالى, I met with Honorable Sheikh Dr Ismail Kassim and received bai'at Qadiriyah Chistiyah.

When I received zikrul anfas from Sheikh Dr Ismail Kassim, I heard in my ears the Kalimah "ALLAH سبحانه و تعالى Hu ALLAH سبحانه و تعالى". I, then realized in myself that the purpose man and genie being created, is to devote ourselves to ALLAH سبحانه و تعالى Rabbul Jalil. With zikirul anfas, I don't feel tired easily

19

when, faced with increasingly complex work routine. My heart can feel the strong bonding to ALLAH سبحانه و تعالى and Rasullullah ﷺ. Understanding of the religion of ALLAH سبحانه و تعالى سبحانه و تعالى and life's direction in this world becomes very clear. Prayer becomes light, more focused at every moment.

I think of ALLAH سبحانه و تعالى سبحانه و تعالى every moment now. I walk through my days expecting the love and forgiveness from ALLAH سبحانه و تعالى سبحانه و تعالى. I'm very temperamental but now I've become more peaceful and relaxed. My thirst for the knowledge of لا إله إلا الله increases more and more. Ya ALLAH سبحانه و تعالى, with your purity and your greatness and your Holy Prophet Muhammad ﷺ, please take us to your side and drown us in your love and care. Amin.

POSTERS AND BANNERS OF PROGRAMS BY
RAHMATAN LIL' ALAMIN ORGANIZATION

From: Central Malaysia

Name: -Withheld- Age: 42 Years
From: Kuala Lumpur

بِسْمِ اللهِ الرَّحْمٰنِ الرَّحِيْمِ
اللّٰهُمَّ صَلِّ عَلَى مُحَمَّدٍ وَعَلَى آلِ مُحَمَّدٍ

فَاعْلَمْ أَنَّهُ لَا إِلَهَ إِلَّا اللَّهُ
وتالله وبالله والله

Thanks to ALLAH سبحانه و تعالى سبحانه و تعالى. I am grateful that I was bestowed with zikrul anfas and bai'at on 21st Rejab 1434 equivalent to 31st May 2013 on a beautiful Friday, full of barakah.

My testimony is from the experience of less than a year, with the qudrat of ALLAH سبحانه و تعالى سبحانه و تعالى and with his power over all things.

The knowledge of ALLAH سبحانه و تعالى Almighty, supersedes the entire universe beyond our understanding, be it within or outside ourselves.

There are some situations of my experience ever since I had zikr anfas that I want to share.

Scientific basis

I get the understanding from the tutoring and barakah of my Mursyid Sheikh Dr Ismail b Hj Kassim and from my early experience that I can use as reference in the practice of zikr anfas and the essence to the world and the hereafter, I will briefly summarize here;

The breath comes from Rabbi al'Alameen, this breath fluctuates from al-hayyat that certainly comes from ALLAH سبحانه و تعالى سبحانه و تعالى to the rest of the Affairs of his creation as a sign of the grandeur of

ALLAH سبحانه و تعالى Almighty which regulates Affairs of his creation. I am very confident that the 'Zikrul anfas ummul zikr' which is the mother of all other zikrs will open secrets of our true self that can only be proved by haqqul yakin and increase our true faith.

Many situations made me tawakuf a while because I was not able to understand in the beginning how this zikir anfas is actually the key, to open and increase spiritual growth. It is difficult to comprehend the experience felt, such a deep secret.

Through zikir anfas we get 'connection' to our creator. For me this is a gift and trust from Rabbul Jalil true, zikr anfas in its hidden knowledge, prompts me to recognize what is said to be the pillar of kalimah syahadah, لا إله إلا الله محمد رسول الله, and the hakikah of RasulALLAH ﷺ سبحانه و تعالى which is the only door towards ALLAH سبحانه و تعالى AlMighty.

Physical benefit

In actual fact, zikrul anfas, if practiced regularly, improves and maintains good health. Physically, I have fully recovered from some disease such as Lung disease and neck problem. In addition, my physical level improved tremendously and I feel healthy. Similarly, I experienced the peace of emotion and mind, better than before. Furthermore, ALLAH سبحانه و تعالى سبحانه و تعالى opens up opportunities, increases and improves my livelihood needs with barakah. In some instances, things that looks impossible to happen, happened, and this makes me more confident to live life, do business successfully.

In spirituality

I do not deny at the early stages of practice of zikir anfas, I was tested in many forms and aspects, be it positive or negative, but in no time, all challenges became good and perfect, and I truly believe that the test is actually a soft "tarbiyah" from ALLAH سبحانه و تعالى Almighty to educate me to recognize the fact of self-realization through, Kalimah لا إله إلا الله and syafaatul Rasulullah ﷺ to achieve true faith (iman). In truth, ALLAH سبحانه و تعالى Almighty has shown Al-Furqan to me and distinguish the right from the wrong, distinguish chains of Satan and the turbulent dirty nafs.

Here I understand many aspects of the proliferation of spirituality that began with zikrul anfas forming between the body and the soul. Without breath, the soul has nothing, no Quwwah. This zikrul anfas transcends asma and zat ALLAH سبحانه و تعالى سبحانه و تعالى that was gifted to us, is actually, a precious secret that cannot be comprehend with common sense, knowledge and the mind.

One thing I feel, with practice of zikrul anfas, also with guidance from sheikh, is that there is communication between mind and qalbu (heart) or spiritual and physical that is difficult to comprehend. In some situations, my soul becomes immersed in the love of ALLAH سبحانه و تعالى and the Messenger..... as if I'm dead but alive, or/ and alive but dead.

With ALLAH سبحانه و تعالى's iftiqar traits and power, ALLAH سبحانه و تعالى سبحانه و تعالى in my life, and after I return or returned all the body, sirr, roh, qalbu and ... or asma, af'al, the nature and substance of ALLAH سبحانه و تعالى Almighty to rightful owner in wajibal wujud, thus the musyahadah with Shahadah and his word can be practiced.

Similarly, it is a purification process also called as "Tazkiyatul nafs". This is my personal pursuit: to identify and achieve the 7 nafs level, by destroying and removing the Nafs Mazmumah, and reaching to the level of obedience with the birth of Nafs Mutmainnah. Ameen, ameen, Ya Rabbal 'Alameen.

This is some of my experience in practice of zikrul anfas, however I feel empty in my heart, I feel I'm still short of faith and piety, it is very necessary to keep practicing muhasabah, muraqabbah and correct my intention itself, with the blessing and guidance from my teachers namely, Maulana Shah Sarkar HabibALLAH سبحانه و تعالى Noori Al-JILANI, Mursyid Sheikh Dr Ismail Kassim, and support of all jemaah. May we all obtain true faith (iman). Ameen ameen, Wasalam.

Salam and al-Fātehah to Qutubul Rabbani, Sheikh Samadani Abdil Qadir Al-Jilani qsa. Sincerely The Spiritual Servant

****

Name: -Withheld-

From: Selayang

بِسْمِ اللهِ الرَّحْمٰنِ الرَّحِيْمِ
اللَّهُمَّ صَلِّ عَلَى مُحَمَّدٍ وَعَلَى آلِ مُحَمَّدٍ
فَاعْلَمْ أَنَّهُ لَا إِلٰهَ إِلَّا اللَّهُ
وتالله وبالله والله

Testimonials: As-Salamu Alaikum, with ALLAH سبحانه
و تعالى's grace and love, on 25th May 2013, I have been bai'at with the zikrul anfas by the respected Sheikh Dr Ismail Kassim. Feels like a newborn again, with unforgettable spiritual and physical experience. Peace that cannot be described with words and imagination. From that moment, being aware and confident that every breath comes and goes back to our creator, I begin to implement the covenant that have been made to ALLAH سبحانه و تعالى سبحانه و تعالى before my birth.

With the permission and blessings of ALLAH و سبحانه تعالى سبحانه و تعالى, the adopting of zikrul anfas and the knowledge لا إله إلا الله and love to his most beloved RasulALLAH ﷺ سبحانه و تعالى, I keep getting serenity and happiness in daily life and in whatever I do. Feels all smooth and beautiful and no stress because in my soul had cultivated a sense of "La Hawla Wala Quwwata Illa Billah". Indeed, the practice of zikrul anfas, I feel my life now very meaningful and I await my time to return to ALLAH سبحانه و تعالى سبحانه و تعالى.

I also hope that the umat of Rasullullah ﷺ can learn and practice zikrul anfas because it is the responsibility of every mukmin. In addition, it could bring us to achieve solihin, humble pray and Solatul Daiem.

****

Name: Shaharel Asyraf
Age: 19 Years
From: Petaling Jaya

بِسْمِ اللهِ الرَّحْمٰنِ الرَّحِيْمِ
اللَّهُمَّ صَلِّ عَلَى مُحَمَّدٍ وَعَلَى آلِ مُحَمَّدٍ
فَاعْلَمْ أَنَّهُ لَا إِلٰهَ إِلَّا اللَّهُ
وتالله وبالله والله

Testimonials: Today is 5th January 2014, I took of Zikr Anfas just around 6 months ago therefore I cannot remember what I experienced and also the fact that I didn't appreciate Zikrul Anfas.

After about 2 months, ALLAH سبحانه و تعالى took away my Zikrul Anfas, I cannot breath with ALLAH Hu ALLAH سبحانه و تعالى, because I didn't appreciate

Zikrul Anfas and I was too caught up with school and friends which turns out to be the distraction that ALLAH سبحانه و تعالى said in Surah An-Nas.

I suffered from a lot of things such as depression and lacked focus in school and studies.

A month later, I regretted, and ALLAH سبحانه و تعالى sent a wali or saint to make me do certain deeds to make me able to breathe with Zikrul Anfas. Once I regain my Zikrul Anfas, my heart felt peaceful and all the distraction was brought down to a minimum.

Alhamdulillah! Zikrul Anfas is the best gift to be given, the riches of the world could not compare to Zikrul Anfas !

****

Sheikh Dr Ismail Kassim Making Doa
On His Visit To Pakistan

Name: Sani Adnan (Ahmad Kamsani Adnan)
Age: 48 Years
From: Selayang, Batu Caves

بِسْمِ اللهِ الرَّحْمٰنِ الرَّحِيْمِ
اللَّهُمَّ صَلِّ عَلَى مُحَمَّدٍ وَعَلَى آلِ مُحَمَّدٍ
فَاعْلَمْ أَنَّهُ لَا إِلٰهَ إِلَّا اللَّهُ
وتالله وبالله والله

Testimonials: Alhamdulillah, after talkin of zikrul anfas, I think less about things which leads to vices, less nightmare dreams although I'm always successful to remove the dream with grace and the help of ALLAH سبحانه و تعالى and peace. I pray that ALLAH و سبحانه تعالى سبحانه و تعالى always support, give the space and time to study, لَا إِلٰهَ إِلَّا اللَّه and knowledge of Syahadah which is the only way to know ALLAH سبحانه و تعالى.

****

Name: ABA
Age: 39 Years
From: Kajang, Selangor

بِسْمِ اللهِ الرَّحْمٰنِ الرَّحِيْمِ
اللَّهُمَّ صَلِّ عَلَى مُحَمَّدٍ وَعَلَى آلِ مُحَمَّدٍ
فَاعْلَمْ أَنَّهُ لَا إِلٰهَ إِلَّا اللَّهُ
وتالله وبالله والله

<u>Testimonials</u>: Alhamdulillah, with Kudrat, Iradat and Permission from ALLAH سبحانه و تعالى, I have been chosen to receive Zikrul

Anfas on 12/12/13. A lot of very significant differences can be felt after the taking of Zikrul Anfas, for example:

1. **Need to be very careful in thinking and intending.**

According to my observations, almost every potential intention will come true even if it is only at a glance in thinking. Among those that can be shared is when by

In the coming of New Year (2014), where, I still don't have a calendar 2014. In my mind, while I was combing my hair, I wished to ALLAH و تعالى سبحانه تعالى that I can get 2014 calendar.

The next day, while walking through the front of a Bank, I heard someone yelled my name. It was an old friend, whom I have not met for a long time. While chatting he gave several sets of 2014 calendar.

A few days after that I received a calendar with the Solat Time as a few weeks earlier I had thought of getting a calendar with Solat time. Masya ALLAH سبحانه و تعالى, 2 weeks after, an organization post to me the calendar that I wanted. The learnings which ALLAH سبحانه و تعالى wanted his servants to understand here is that to always rely on ALLAH سبحانه و تعالى and remove "one self".

No matter how small the matter is, because we are "La Hawla Wala" - we have no power. In truth, we cannot even blink our eyes at all except with kudrat of ALLAH سبحانه و تعالى. When everything is submitted to ALLAH سبحانه و تعالى's, then only the movement of the us is "movement" of ALLAH سبحانه و تعالى, our hearing is the "hearing" of ALLAH سبحانه و تعالى, Our vision is "sight" of ALLAH سبحانه و تعالى and our "needs" is the needs of ALLAH سبحانه و تعالى. When everything's or Iradat ALLAH سبحانه و تعالى, how can ALLAH سبحانه و تعالى refuse to accept our prayers. Only by thorough understanding of the knowledge of Tauhidul Zat, Properties, Asma' and Af'al, which is part of the knowledge of Kalimah لَا إِلَهَ إِلَّا اللَّه, we are able to appreciate, enjoy and most importantly "Syahadah" at all the attributes of ALLAH سبحانه و تعالى.

2. **All negativity, disease, mazmumah and batil will be removed gradually and "Ulluhiyah attributes" which is already "embedded" at each Individual also will be radiating**

Little by little through sharper thinking, speech that is always knowledgeable, hungry for knowledge and avoid things that is meaningless. All of which, happened naturally and never forced nor acted. Our internal sensors becomes sharper in the detection of what is batil and haq especially when faced with many variety and types of people.

3. **Feel always in the care and tutelage of ALLAH** سبحانه و تعالى **SUBḤĀNAHU WA TA'ĀLA**. ALLAH سبحانه و تعالى inspires and pours spiritual knowledge through the events that occurred in our environment. It is up to us to capture and understand the knowledge behind it. The most important reference is our mursyid to guide us in opening up our spiritual experience so that we do not go astray due to the deception of Satan.

4. **Feel as if there is an energy that acts as a shield to block all the false, negativity and mazmumah from approaching us and family**.

It is up to the individual to program this energy. However, as humans, we are not free from being complacent/default and at times this shield would open up and we are exposed to the attacks of the devil, jin and satan.

Previously, before we had zikrul anfas, maybe the attack comes from low ranking army of satan like *Corporal* or *Private* but now after having zikrul anfas, the high ranking or special force, the likes of sergeant or admiral. Then of course, the tactics of his attacks are also different.

Let's together constantly upgrade and equipped ourselves with sophisticated weapons, that is the Kaliamah لَا إِلَهَ إِلَّا اللَّه.

- ABA – 28 January 2014 (Tuesday)

Name: Azian Rashid
Age: 45 Years
From: Petaling Jaya

بِسْمِ اللهِ الرَّحْمنِ الرَّحِيْمِ
اللَّهُمَّ صَلِّ عَلَى مُحَمَّدٍ وَعَلَى آلِ مُحَمَّدٍ
فَاعْلَمْ أَنَّهُ لَا إِلَهَ إِلَّا اللَّهُ
وتالله وبالله والله

<u>Testimonials</u>: In summary, differences found before and after zikr anfas. I found that it is an effective tool as:

Payment reminders alert: I realized that my zikrul anfas kicked in when I was faced with "negative" actions.

That reminded you of what is right or wrong. If you are faced with "wrong" actions, you quickly ask for forgiveness - Istighfar. If you are faced with positive actions – you are awed by the Power of AlMighty ALLAH سبحانه و تعالى, and overwhelmed by the Love that HE has given you.

Syifa: at times, when I desperately needed a quick fix, remedy for my illness, I simply do my Zikrul Anfas. I have not been taking my cough syrup for my cough, and taking in, fewer to none, pills to get over my migraine.

Blessings/Provision: Wishes do come true. 2 weeks after receiving Zikrul Anfas. I had to present a project to get endorsement from my boss during a public holiday. I wished/prayed for a quick and successful presentation. True enough, it went like a breeze, and I got the endorsement within 30mins.

However, the twist to that is, I realized that you have <u>to be careful of what you think, or wish for</u>. Sometimes, a mere simple thought or utterance like I wish I can get a parking lot, or like I want another cup of coffee can materialize in split second. You might get your wish to something that resulted in detrimental effects, or give the different result than you would have liked. And, it was too late to undo.

Hence, I had learn to be calmer or level headed and hold any negative thoughts/comments in order to avoid making unnecessary assumptions/thoughts or comments that could lead to perceived negative results for yourself or other parties.

****

Name: Edrus Hafizi Abdul Razak
Age: 44 Years
From: Damansara Damai, Selangor

بِسْمِ اللهِ الرَّحْمٰنِ الرَّحِيْمِ
اللَّهُمَّ صَلِّ عَلَى مُحَمَّدٍ وَعَلَى آلِ مُحَمَّدٍ
فَاعْلَمْ أَنَّهُ لَا إِلٰهَ إِلَّا اللَّهُ
وتاللّه وباللّه واللّه

Testimonials: I received Zikrul Anfas on August 2013. Unlike other jemaah who received some amazing experiences during talqin of Zikrul Anfas, I just felt a sense of peace present in the heart. After a while I noticed a vibrational feeling along breath inhaled and exhaled. This vibration increased when I was in the Majlis of Ilm and Zikr where sometimes my fingertips also vibrates. The most significant change I have experienced after receiving Zikrul anfas is when doing prayers. Last time, I had too much disturbance in my prayers. Mind drifting away, felt unsure and sometimes forgot what rakaat I was in during prayers. Now my prayers feels more khusyu'. I feel as if ALLAH سبحانه و

تعالى Subhana Wa'Taala is in front of me and made me feel more tawadu'. Syukoor to the grace of ALLAH سبحانه و تعالى Subhana Wa'taala this heart feels more peaceful.

****

Name: -Withheld-
Age: 39 Years
From: Kuala Lumpur

بِسْمِ اللهِ الرَّحْمٰنِ الرَّحِيْمِ
اللَّهُمَّ صَلِّ عَلَى مُحَمَّدٍ وَعَلَى آلِ مُحَمَّدٍ
فَاعْلَمْ أَنَّهُ لَا إِلٰهَ إِلَّا اللَّهُ
وتالله وبالله والله

Testimonials: Having put this lost knowledge into practice, I must say that the direct connection to ALLAH سبحانه و تعالى via *zikrul anfas* has enhanced my faith in Him alone-in spite of the increasingly atheistic, paganised and ailing world. At the same time, the inner self becomes more frequent composed with the awareness of His Presence.

Name: Hadi Iskandar
Age: 19 Years
From: Petaling Jaya, Selangor

بِسْمِ اللهِ الرَّحْمٰنِ الرَّحِيْمِ
اللَّهُمَّ صَلِّ عَلَى مُحَمَّدٍ وَعَلَى آلِ مُحَمَّدٍ

فَاعْلَمْ أَنَّهُ لَا إِلَهَ إِلَّا اللَّهُ

وتاللّه وبالله والله

Testimonials: After getting my zikrul anfas, immediately i felt calm and alhamdu lillah, i feel connected to ALLAH سبحانه و تعالى. Before this, i didnt want to take zikrul anfas, but 'WALLAH سبحانه و تعالى' getting it is incredibly magnificent. It is to a point where if possible I just want to be around mu'mins and my murshid only. Getting zikrul anfas has increased my yaqin, my love and basically all those that I've never felt towards ALLAH سبحانه و تعالى and the Prophet ﷺ to a whole new level.

****

Name: Jefri Razali

Age: 48 Years

From: Kuala Lumpur

بِسْمِ اللّهِ الرَّحْمٰنِ الرَّحِيْمِ

اللّٰهُمَّ صَلِّ عَلَى مُحَمَّدٍ وَعَلَى آلِ مُحَمَّدٍ

فَاعْلَمْ أَنَّهُ لَا إِلَهَ إِلَّا اللَّهُ

وتاللّه وبالله والله

Testimonials: After receiving the zikrul anfas from honorable Sheikh on last Ramadan, I found my prayers more Khusyu'. I feel the relationship between me with ALLAH سبحانه و تعالى exist every time I pray. I can feel the presence and attention of ALLAH سبحانه و تعالى in my doa after prayer and the sweetness of the prayer that I could not describe.

I am pressured with business every day, I often wake up at night feeling hot in the vicinity of my chest (heart burn) up to a point I have to sit for a moment to ease the pain. Alhamdulillah, after practicing zikrul anfas, the stress is gone. It is a great remedy for the soul. All problems can be resolved one by one.

A lot more of zikrul anfas benefit but could not be shared here. Gratitude to ALLAH سبحانه و تعالى because he met me with the honorable Sheikh. I wish our honorable Sheikh is always in the blessing of ALLAH سبحانه و تعالى Almighty. Ameen.

****

Name: Mohamad Haziff Bin Hamzah
Age: 48 Years
From: Wangsa Maju, Kuala Lumpur

بِسْمِ اللهِ الرَّحْمٰنِ الرَّحِيْمِ
اللَّهُمَّ صَلِّ عَلَى مُحَمَّدٍ وَعَلَى آلِ مُحَمَّدٍ
فَاعْلَمْ أَنَّهُ لَا إِلٰهَ إِلَّا اللَّهُ
وتالله وبالله والله

Testimonials: *In The Name Of ALLAH* سبحانه و تعالى, *Most Gracious Most Merciful*

Be grateful, with his bounty and by his mercy Guide to learn his knowledge to know *ALLAH* سبحانه و تعالى. Surely *ALLAH* سبحانه و تعالى *is the creator of* worlds in the heavens and the Earth.

I am grateful for the grace of *ALLAH* سبحانه و تعالى سبحانه و تعالى for giving me Hidayah by meeting me with my Mursyid Al-Faqir Ill ALLAH سبحانه و تعالى Sheikh Dr Ismail Kassim to learn knowledge extremely valuable and extremely vast to know *ALLAH و* سبحانه تعالى. After Bai'at and received Zikrul Anfas through my Mursyid Al-Faqir Ill ALLAH سبحانه و تعالى Sheikh Dr Ismail Kassim, I cried witnessing the greatness of *ALLAH* سبحانه و تعالى, understood that I am only his slaves and I have no power at all. For now I'm proud of what I have but in reality, all won't be permanent and does not have any power except by the will of *ALLAH* سبحانه و تعالى سبحانه و تعالى.

Followed by receiving zikrul anfas, the heart is open in learning knowledge of *ALLAH* سبحانه و تعالى سبحانه و تعالى. Indeed I am only his slaves, who must worship to *ALLAH* سبحانه و تعالى and surrender everything to *ALLAH* سبحانه و تعالى.

Previously, performing prayers were heavy for me. If, and when I do it, my mind would drift to mundane thoughts. Never enough with what sustenance I earned, I always complained about current problems. I am hot tempered, easily agitated, that even my kids avoided me.

On the other hand, I find peace by wasting time with my friends outside. I would expect help from creations such as money, worldly asset and friends.

Alhamdullilah, I am grateful to the grace of *ALLAH* سبحانه و تعالى, after receiving the Zikrul anfas and learn the knowledge of *ALLAH* سبحانه و تعالى, I did it all because of *ALLAH* سبحانه و تعالى سبحانه و تعالى. Indeed, I was his slave and to *ALLAH* سبحانه و تعالى I ask from. Doing prayers is not at all heavy but peaceful in my life. In fact I came to fear *ALLAH* سبحانه و تعالى if *ALLAH* سبحانه و تعالى does not want to see me and I am afraid of becoming a kufur. The kids were closer to me, they are not afraid of me but seek me. My wife cried of joy with what I did today. I am sure she is also grateful to *ALLAH* سبحانه و تعالى سبحانه و تعالى with his mercy of givng Hidayah to me. Alhamdullilah, my life today is more relaxed than in the past. I always pray to *ALLAH* سبحانه و تعالى سبحانه و تعالى to give me strength in learning this knowledge so that I can bring my family to the blessed path of ALLAH و سبحانه سبحانه و تعالى تعالى. Amin.

Aceh. Indonesia – Sheikh Dr Ismail Kassim
Interview With Radio Seulaweut 91Fm

Name: Mohd Muhaimin
Age: -undisclosed-
From: Ampang, Kuala Lumpur

بِسْمِ اللهِ الرَّحْمٰنِ الرَّحِيْمِ
اللَّهُمَّ صَلِّ عَلَى مُحَمَّدٍ وَعَلَى آلِ مُحَمَّدٍ
فَاعْلَمْ أَنَّهُ لَا إِلٰهَ إِلَّا اللّٰهُ
وتالله وبالله والله

Testimonials:

1. FEELING AFTER GETTING ZIKRUL ANFAS

Answer: after getting zikrul anfas, moments after being talqin-ed by Sheikh Dr Ismail Kassim, I felt calm.... no more random voices on ears & as soon as received zikrul anfas. I feel my chest beating & back to normal again.

2. DAILY LIFE AFTER GETTING ZIKRUL ANFAS

Answer: Life is calm, especially when doing zikrul anfas. Inhale 'ALLAH سبحانه و تعالى', Exhale 'Hu' deeper and stable. Especially voices of Satan and nafs is decreasing ... presumably the sorts of 60%-70% reduced. Now 30% disruption. This is very helpful for prayers and focused attention, and increased self-confidence, especially during zikrul anfas. I am more confident confronting other people now because there I have a connection with ALLAH سبحانه و تعالى Azza Wa Jalla, through Zikrul Anfas. Alhamdulillah.

Name: Mohd Rashidan
Age: 48 Years
From: Petaling Jaya

بِسْمِ اللهِ الرَّحْمٰنِ الرَّحِيْمِ
اللَّهُمَّ صَلِّ عَلَى مُحَمَّدٍ وَعَلَى آلِ مُحَمَّدٍ
فَاعْلَمْ أَنَّهُ لَا إِلٰهَ إِلَّا اللَّهُ
وتالله وبالله والله

Testimonials: Alhamdulillah, Praises to ALLAH سبحانه و تعالى AlMighty and Peace to our most beloved Prophet Muhammad ﷺ, his family, his progeny and his companions and to our Mashaikh Sultanul Aulia Sheikh Abdul Qadir AlJailani qsa.

I was bestowed with Zikrul anfas at Ajmer, India. The blessed place of our Mashaikh Khaja Moinuddin Chisti Sultanul Hind. Zikr of the breath is the greatest gift that ALLAH سبحانه و تعالى AlMighty has given to his

43

servants and honestly to me, this is more precious than any jewels or diamonds in this world even more precious than this life itself. I remember during the bai'at, Iqrar along with Sarkar and Sheikh Dr Ismail Kassim, I was feeling elated and happiest. One of the best moment of my life.

I recall back then, during the start of Talqin of Zikr of the breath, Sheikh told us to breath slowly and peacefully and clear away all thoughts, that was in our mind. As the Talqin was a full-blown to my ears, I was breathing normally for the first few minutes. Suddenly there was a burst of energy and the force of current running through my chest, my breathing started to become stronger, harder and frenetic. My body started to tremble, I felt strong energy flowing through my body and finally my hands hardened and stiffen and could not move. I cried during that time and then I saw a light in front of me and my breathing gradually slowed down and I felt tranquility and peace in my heart, so cool inside. Later, I was awaken and greeted by Sheikh Dr Ismail Kassim and all our entourage who was there with us.

Now, 4 months have passed and there are changes that I feel in me. Just to name a few, 1) My prayers is more focused, deep and meaningful. 2) My heart feels tranquil and peace. 3) Sometimes I can just burst into tears when I think of ALLAH سبحانه و تعالى's grace to us or when thoughts of our beloved Propeht Muhammad

ﷺ comes to me. 4) My Zikrul anfas can be felt regularly, especially so when I do the Syahadah. And now with the 40 minutes of Zikrul anfas, I practice doing daily, I can feel the current and vibration resonating through my body quite regularly.

Alhamdulillah, I pray that we be connected to ALLAH سبحانه و تعالى and our Holy Prophet Muhammad ﷺ all the time until we die. And with Zikrul anfas we are always connected. AMEEN.

Aceh. Indonesia - Sheikh Dr Ismail Kassim
Visit To Prasentren Naqshabandi

Name: Mohd Razali Bin Mohd Salleh
Age: -undisclosed-
From: Rawang, Selangor

بِسْمِ اللهِ الرَّحْمٰنِ الرَّحِيْمِ
اللَّهُمَّ صَلِّ عَلَى مُحَمَّدٍ وَعَلَى آلِ مُحَمَّدٍ
فَاعْلَمْ أَنَّهُ لَا إِلٰهَ إِلَّا اللَّهُ
وتالله وبالله والله

45

I am Mohd Razali B Mohd Salleh from Country Homes, Rawang.

Here, I want to share my experience after five (5) months of practicing Zikrul Anfas.

Our prayers become more focused because we feel confident in ALLAH سبحانه و تعالى and the spirit to pray grows because we realize that we are meeting the King, a true King who is All-knowing of our pleasures and trouble, very merciful and loving us.

Zikr is like a fortress to us, we are only aware of the fortress when it is opened or exposed due to our forgetfulness to the zikr. Satan and nafs will disturb at that moment to bring disarray to our thoughts and our hearts.

Zikrul Anfas will also strengthen our confidence in ALLAH سبحانه و تعالى because ALLAH سبحانه و تعالى will provide help and advice when we seek Him.

This is how much I can share within 5 months of experience of doing zikrul anfas. I could not narrate more completely because of the enormous benefits of this zikrul anfas. May ALLAH سبحانه و تعالى sustains this connection and opens all doors to the "noor" of ALLAH سبحانه و تعالى and the Messenger's filled in this self.

Wassalam

****

Name: -Withheld-
Age: -undisclosed-
From: Selangor

بِسْمِ اللهِ الرَّحْمٰنِ الرَّحِيْمِ
اللَّهُمَّ صَلِّ عَلَىٰ مُحَمَّدٍ وَعَلَىٰ آلِ مُحَمَّدٍ
فَاعْلَمْ أَنَّهُ لَا إِلٰهَ إِلَّا اللَّهُ
وتالله وبالله والله

Testimonials: All Praise Be to ALLAH سبحانه و تعالى, illa of the worlds.

I am grateful because ALLAH سبحانه و تعالى has chosen me to write this testimony, I'll share what I can. Before attending the ceremony of remembrance(zikir), I was determined to strengthen the zikrul anfas and I would like to bolster my confidence in ALLAH سبحانه و تعالى which over the years my confidence in ALLAH سبحانه و تعالى has weakened. After I attended the camp for 3 days 2 nights I received a very big impact in myself - that I could feel the greatness of ALLAH سبحانه و تعالى in my life. I could feel and I could see via the senses that ALLAH سبحانه و تعالى has given me, I could feel each and every creature of ALLAH سبحانه و تعالى has no power but come from the power of ALLAH سبحانه و تعالى, the Almighty. I got a sense of peace that I have never felt before. I feel very grateful to ALLAH سبحانه و تعالى because ALLAH سبحانه و تعالى has given me a teacher who is close to ALLAH سبحانه و تعالى. When Sheikh Ismail Kassim teaches knowledge of لَا إِلَهَ إِلَّا اللَّه, I can feel this knowledge is very useful in my life because it taught me tauheed to ALLAH سبحانه و تعالى, The Only One.

When we deny there's no Illah besides ALLAH سبحانه و تعالى in our lives, I could feel in my life all of which is created is and consist the love of ALLAH سبحانه و تعالى to his creations. When we always adopt the Syahadah which we deny there are lesser deities except ALLAH سبحانه و تعالى. Heart and our faith will be more strong and confident to ALLAH سبحانه و تعالى. This the kind of faith that was present among the companions-Sahabah of Rasulullah ﷺ in which their confidence is very strong in ALLAH سبحانه و تعالى. Once we have strong iman (faith) in ALLAH سبحانه و تعالى, every element, for example, our breath must be submitted in the name of ALLAH سبحانه و تعالى and returned back to us with the name of ALLAH سبحانه و تعالى. Only then, our hearts shall always remember ALLAH سبحانه و تعالى, Satan could not disturb by the will of ALLAH سبحانه و تعالى.

When I practise Zikrul anfas I was able to feel the peace of soul and I feel ALLAH سبحانه و تعالى so close to me. I felt I was like a new baby born with no sin. Zikrul anfas affects me where my heart always remember

ALLAH سبحانه و تعالى all the time and I feel sad when I forget ALLAH سبحانه و تعالى. Once again I am grateful and thankful to ALLAH سبحانه و تعالى, the Almighty ALLAH سبحانه و تعالى show me to the right path. Thank You ALLAH سبحانه و تعالى, Assalamualaikum.

****

Name: Noorshima
Age: -undisclosed-
From: Selangor

بِسْمِ اللهِ الرَّحْمٰنِ الرَّحِيْمِ
اللَّهُمَّ صَلِّ عَلَى مُحَمَّدٍ وَعَلَى آلِ مُحَمَّدٍ
فَاعْلَمْ أَنَّهُ لَا إِلٰهَ إِلَّا اللَّهُ
وتالله وبالله والله

Testimonial: Zikr of the breath, Relationship to the creator I, received the zikr of the breath on September 2013. Thanks to the grace of ALLAH سبحانه و تعالى Almighty on the favors.

My experience, I have just received my zikrul anfas and overall it is remarkable.

What I have found, the notion, the realization when I'm in the state of forgetfulness to ALLAH سبحانه و تعالى, Zikrul anfas has become sort of a tool that reminds me of the importance in remembering ALLAH سبحانه و تعالى and Rasul ﷺ. In addition, when I'm with the jamaah or in a ceremony (majlis), my zikrul anfas moves easily, especially in the presence of Sheikh or ceremony of mawlid with Sheikh's jamaah.

I am also grateful, because my husband is now practicing the zikrul anfas. Unintentionally, we feel the importance of "tarbiyah" to educate and encourage in particular, my children, family and others to get a valid true faith teachings.

At one point, before, I felt disconnected from the events of knowledge and zikr. Now, I feel much closer, Alhamdu lillah.

Another point that have become the reason for my pursuit of Iman is Patience. Proven in one of the verses in the Quran; InnaALLAH سبحانه و تعالى ma'a Sabiriin, (indeed ALLAH سبحانه و تعالى is with the patience) in relation to the context, by doing zikrul anfas, I feel close to the feel of patience and I can accomplish a lot of things in a day. Whether or not, it is this world or the hereafter, I can walk with patience and calm. Emotionally, I look fair and secure. SubhanaALLAH سبحانه و تعالى.

From the teachings of Sheikh, summarizing what I understand is that, zikrul anfas relates a lot to Kalimah لَا إِلَهَ إِلَّا اللَّه. In the chapter of nafi isbat (deny and conforming) and Ya Hayyu Ya Qayyum, inhaling Ya

Hayyu and exhaling Ya Qayyum. Ilmu kalimah of syahadah is the root to the amal of zikrul nafas.

Indirectly, this shows the great power and the sovereignty of ALLAH سبحانه و تعالى, controlling his creations. We have no power at all. La Hawla Wa La Quwata illa Billahil aliyil Azhim

With the awareness that, certainly the level of dependency we have towards ALLAH سبحانه و تعالى سبحانه و تعالى will increase and thus feel the sweetness of real tawheed.

However, I still need istiqamah to strengthen this practice that will ultimately build goodness in dunia and the hereafter by a faith and devotion.

Ameen Ameen Yes Rbbal Alameen, wassalam

****

Aceh. Indonesia - Sheikh Dr Ismail Kassim
Visit To Prasentren Naqshabandi

****

Name: Dr Khadijah Md Jadi
Age: 51 Years
From: Bangi, Selangor

بِسْمِ اللهِ الرَّحْمٰنِ الرَّحِيْمِ
اللَّهُمَّ صَلِّ عَلَى مُحَمَّدٍ وَعَلَى آلِ مُحَمَّدٍ
فَاعْلَمْ أَنَّهُ لَا إِلَهَ إِلَّا اللَّهُ
وتالله وبالله والله

Testimonials:

1. My experience in the acceptance of zikrul anfas. Taken on 12th December 2013.

Upon the bai'at of zikr anfas, I see the nur of the sifat of ALLAH سبحانه و تعالى in the eyes of Sheikh. This is relating to the saying it is not Sheikh that is looking but ALLAH سبحانه و تعالى

Only ALLAH سبحانه و تعالى knew what I felt.... I felt so emotional and every time I look at shiekh's face. I become more emotional that I wish that ALLAH سبحانه و تعالى will give me strong faith.

A feeling like electric shock coursing through the body and specifically, the hands, as if, the ruh or soul is about to leave my body. Feeling of fear was also present.

I couldn't contain the feeling of sadness. It is very strong each time I do my syahadah anfas and sirr. Ya ALLAH سبحانه و تعالى! We own nothing, not even our ruh.

2. Feeling very calm and loving towards ALLAH سبحانه و تعالى, and also feeling how much ALLAH سبحانه و تعالى loves me. This feeling cannot be replaced with anything in this world. The feeling of ALLAH سبحانه و تعالى being in the breath and sirr. ALLAH سبحانه و تعالى is so close with us.

3. Solat is more khusuk syahadah is very easy with the presence of zikrul anfas.

4. Dependence on ALLAH سبحانه و تعالى is stronger ... with suspension of breath and ruh ALLAH سبحانه و تعالى at zat

Name: Hasmah Ali
Age: 43 Years
From: Templer Saujana, Selangor

بِسْمِ اللهِ الرَّحْمٰنِ الرَّحِيْمِ
اللَّهُمَّ صَلِّ عَلَى مُحَمَّدٍ وَعَلَى آلِ مُحَمَّدٍ
فَاعْلَمْ أَنَّهُ لَا إِلٰهَ إِلَّا اللَّهُ
وتاللهِ وباللهِ واللهِ

Testimonials: To write and share about zikrul anfas, the ink for this pen will not be enough. I have been practicing zikrul anfas for almost 1 year. My previous testimony has been submitted and published in the earlier publication of this book. What I would like to share here, may be of a help to others to reinforce the importance of zikrul anfas, and to use the zikrul anfas not just to gain peace.

My experience is when I was invited to the country's largest prison. I was there to visit my Muslim brothers and sisters. It was my first time, and it had me confused and scared. Immediately, I did my zikrul anfas and all the mentioned feeling was gone. The point here is, Zikrul anfas makes every hard or difficult task becomes easy.

InsyaALLAH سبحانه و تعالى.

****

Name: Maryam Abdul Razak
Age: -undisclosed-
From: Rawang, Selangor

بِسْمِ اللهِ الرَّحْمٰنِ الرَّحِيْمِ
اللَّهُمَّ صَلِّ عَلَى مُحَمَّدٍ وَعَلَى آلِ مُحَمَّدٍ
فَاعْلَمْ أَنَّهُ لَا إِلٰهَ إِلَّا اللَّهُ
وتالله وبالله والله

Testimonials: Assalamualaikum, for the grace and love to ALLAH سبحانه و تعالى for he has brought me to the discovery of Rahmatan Lil' Alamin Organization(Perahmat).

The first time I saw Sheikh Dr Ismail Kassim was on Youtube. The talkin of Zikrul Anfas really caught my interest because I have been looking for ways to remember ALLAH سبحانه و تعالى in a genuine way. After watching several videos of Sheikh Dr Ismail Kassim on Youtube, I decided to meet Sheikh and the jamaah of Rahmatan Lil'Alamin Organization.

On 16th January, 2014 I took bai'at and Zikrul Anfas through Sheikh Dr Ismail Kassim at Pulau Besar, Melaka. After receiving my zikrul anfas, I felt as though I have entered a new phase in life; like my life has only just begun.

Unlike before, I have been looking for the real meaning of life as a servant of ALLAH سبحانه و تعالى. Before bestowed with Zikrul Anfas, I never felt content with my life, my life seemed incomplete. After bestowed with Zikrul Anfas, I started feeling a kind of peace that is hard to describe. Before, I was easily stressed out and angry. However, after receiving Zikrul anfas, I found it difficult to get angry. It was obvious, in my relationship with the jamaah of Rahmatan Lil' Alamin Organization, I felt countless bond of love existed between them. Being a part of the Rahmatan Lil'Alamin Organization family is the greatest blessing from ALLAH سبحانه و تعالى. Gratitude to ALLAH سبحانه و تعالى for placing me here with the jamaah of Rahmatan Lil' Alamin Organization and many thanks to Sheikh as well as the jamaah.

Thank you, thank you.

****

Name: -Withheld-
Age: -undisclosed-
From: Selangor

بِسْمِ اللهِ الرَّحْمنِ الرَّحِيْمِ
اللَّهُمَّ صَلِّ عَلَى مُحَمَّدٍ وَعَلَى آلِ مُحَمَّدٍ
فَاعْلَمْ أَنَّهُ لَا إِلَهَ إِلَّا اللَّهُ
وتالله وبالله والله

Testimonials: Assalamu'alaikum.

The first time I met Sheikh Dr. Ismail Hj Kassim (Sheikh) was on 23rd April 2013, after Maghrib at Madrasah Al Sheikh Abdul Qadir Jilani, Rawang (Madrasah). I was bestowed with Zikrul Anfas (*Qadariah wa Chistiyah Order*) on 18 Ramadan 1434H (27.7.2013) before breaking fast in Madrasah by Sheikh.

1. The most obvious effect from the practice of zikrul anfas on me is, improved focus in prayers compared to before I took baiah. I notice, it is now easy for me to be closer to ALLAH سبحانه و تعالى in prayers rather than using method taught in books and kitabs that simply asks us to remember the meaning of our recitals to make presence of khusyuk.

2. The second effect is, I see some positive change in my daily lives. For example, love to pray in the early hours, love and easy to pray with the family together (home only), Not burdened to do the sunat practices (amal) as well as easy to accept the test by looking at that all testings and resistance is coming from ALLAH سبحانه و تعالى.

3. I also noticed that my daily life routines becomes systematically well and in order. The responsibility and environment is good while family affairs gets even better, as I hold responsibility as head of the family. Alhamdulillah, I always think of ways to thank Sheikh

and I always pray that Sheikh's has long life and in good health, in particular to spread knowledge of the Kalimah لَا إِلٰهَ إِلَّا اللَّه.

Name: Dr Yahya Muhammad
Age: 63 Years
From: Cheras, Kuala Lumpur

بِسْمِ اللهِ الرَّحْمٰنِ الرَّحِيْمِ
اللَّهُمَّ صَلِّ عَلَى مُحَمَّدٍ وَعَلَى آلِ مُحَمَّدٍ
فَاعْلَمْ أَنَّهُ لَا إِلٰهَ إِلَّا اللَّهُ
وتالله وبالله والله

<u>Testimonials</u>: Practitioners of Zikrul anfas over the last 5 years

Achievements & True Practitioners

Zikrul anfas was something alien for all my life born as a Muslim to the ripe age of 63 because I never knew these words from any 'alim that I had learned from since the age of 10 or earlier. Until to this day, many alims appear not to know or do not want to express their opinion on this aspect of ilmu on zikirullah.

This is strange as ALLAH سبحانه و تعالى enjoins zikir as part of the important 'amal of the mukmins as stated in many ayaat of Al Quran. In particular the ayah 7 of Surah Al 'Araf (7:205) "wazkur robbaka fi nafsika" (And remember your Robb in yourself...) is related to the zikirul anfaas. Indeed, when I came to realize on this subject, it is not strange at all as to why ordinary alims (alim al kitab or alim al syariah) cannot convey this aspect of the ilmu. Actually, there are two channels of ilmu. One is related to ilmu of Islam and syariah, the other is the ilmu of spirituality which includes ilmu of iman, tauheed, qalbu, nafs, roh, et cetera. These are ilmu ghaib related to the third ayah in Surah Al Baqarah. This group of ilmu is generally known as ilmu hikmah (about wisdom), ilmu haqiqat (about knowing the reality) and ilmu makrifat (about knowing ALLAH سبحانه و تعالى). All these ilmu can only be learned under لا إله إلا الله as directed by ALLAH سبحانه و تعالى in ayah 19 of Surah Muhammad (47:19). Both channels of the ilmu and ammal of these ilmu are derived from Al Quran and Al Hadith, and As Sunnah.

However, the second category of the ilmu and ammal can only be transmitted by the people selected by ALLAH سبحانه و تعالى to give such knowledge. This group of people includes the ambiya (prophets) and awlyia (wali ALLAH سبحانه و تعالى of arief billah status) as confirmed by Al Quran in Surah Al Baqarah (2:269) and Surah Al Ankabut (29:49).

The experience of zikrul anfas came into reality after I took ba'iat from a great Murshid from whom the zikr was "talqeen" (prompted by breathing voices) into my ears by Sheikh Dr. Ismail bin Hj. Kassim on the directive of the Murshid Sarkar. My Sheikh or Sarkar is of the status Sultanul Ariffin. He is Sheikh Syed Muhammad Noorullah Shah Ariefuddin Al Jilani (QSA) of the Golden Chain of salsilah which connects to Rasullullah ﷺ through Saidina Ali رضي الله عنه and Fatimah Al Zahrah رضي الله عنها, Imam Hassan and Iman Hussein, رضي الله عنه, and through many generations of the Sultanul Awlyia Sheikh Abdul Kadir Al Jailani (QSA).

Sarkar is the 23rd grandson of the Sultanul Awlyia. This "isnad" (historiography) of the transmission of this branch of ilmu is very important criteria for the transmission of such "ilmu ghaib" which otherwise cannot be obtained through other channels. And thus the right way or the straight path cannot be found except through the rightly guided teachers as stated in Al Quran regarding walyyan murshida (Surah Al Kahfi, 18:17).

In a spiritual sense, zikrul anfas is the unbreakable "Rope of ALLAH سبحانه و تعالى" or "Hablillah" as mentioned in Al Quran (Surah Ali Imran, 3:103). Zikrul anfas is a very powerful "gift" from ALLAH سبحانه و تعالى that is directed to be used for the control of negative nafs and whispers of the jinns and annas, especially in solat. Based on my personal experience, I can confirm that it is not very possible to achieve a good khusyu' if I do not apply the zikrul anfas in solat. In daily life, the amal of zikrul anfas connects our deep kolbu and roh to ALLAH سبحانه و تعالى. Zikrul anfas enables me to achieve a sustainable sense of connection and "closeness and personal relation" with ALLAH سبحانه و تعالى. Whether we experience it consciously or unconsciously, we will certainly get the inner peace that every human being needs but could not have it through any other ways. What is more important than inner peace and remembrance of your Robb, ALLAH سبحانه و تعالى, the One and the Only Creator? And this is easily achieved through the practice of zikrul anfas. You need to experience it to understand what zikrul anfas is because words cannot explain the reality of zikrul anfas.

****

Name: Datin Surayati Othman
Age: 59 Years
From: Selangor

بِسْمِ اللهِ الرَّحْمٰنِ الرَّحِيْمِ
اللَّهُمَّ صَلِّ عَلَى مُحَمَّدٍ وَعَلَى آلِ مُحَمَّدٍ
فَاعْلَمْ أَنَّهُ لَا إِلَٰهَ إِلَّا اللَّهُ
وتالله وبالله والله

فَاعْلَمْ أَنَّهُ لَا إِلَٰهَ إِلَّا اللَّهُ وَاسْتَغْفِرْ لِذَنبِكَ وَلِلْمُؤْمِنِينَ وَالْمُؤْمِنَاتِ
Muhammad 47:19 وَاللَّهُ يَعْلَمُ مُتَقَلَّبَكُمْ وَمَثْوَاكُمْ-

'Wamaa 'arsalnaaka Ilaa Rahmatan Lil 'alameen"

Assalamualaikum

My name is Surayati Othman born in 18 April 1955. I am a muslim activist and advocate of animals' Right and nature environment and ecology in the Islamic perspective. I am very much inspired to create awareness and educate our muslims community of sharing ALLAH سبحانه و تعالى's Ikhsan/Compassion/Mercy and Wisdom granted to His creatures animals, living things and nature eco-environment obligatory through practice of dakwah bil haal.

I was bestowed zikirul anfas on the 25th May 2013 in the tranquil and spiritual Island of Pulau Besar by my Guru Mursyid Sheikh Dr Ismail Kassim who was also once a good friend and brother whom I have known for the past 15 years. He was the one who helped me when I needed help and at the time I was truely down in life. He was the first person who raised up his hand when I solicit for a personal computer to help me in my dakwah work when nobody did. When I needed financial help to solve my matrimonial legal fees he assisted without any slightest qualm or hesitation. For all he did as a kind and sincere soul.

ALLAH سبحانه و تعالى bestowed the Zikrul Anfas upon me His humble servant through him, (an honorary of the world and the Herafter) and from the golden chains of Prophethood of Nabi Muhammads ﷺ and the Purity of the Grand Awliya Sultanul Shiekh Abdul Qadir Jilani and his decendents of the present Sheikh Sarkar of Hyderabad.

When i was about 12 years old I dreamed of our beloved Prophet Muhammad ﷺ in white robe with his white beard lying on his bed in his last breadth as someone stabbed him from the back. I saw me kissing his hand. Ironically, I thought i saw the same figure of him in the dawn sky above the Holy Kaabah of Mecca during an umrah trip during Ramadhan some years ago. All these strange incidents did make me to wonder if the grace of being granted Zikrul Anfas has indeed unfolded the Signs of what ALLAH سبحانه و تعالى's Will and Leave.

InnALLAH yehdi men yesha. "ALLAH guides whom He will!" Indeed ALLAH سبحانه و تعالى has rewarded me with the blessing of bringing 6 souls to the light of Islam of whom one was my late husband Muhammad Azneill Mckay Ross. Alhamdulillah! But ma ana bikhari.... I am not learned...

I consider myself as ignorant as a convert or a revert. Though a shariah compliant I have a weakness in the Koran literacy and still in the study. Acquiring the priceless Ilmu of Iman and Kalimah Shahadah has indeed paved me the way to the Path of ALLAH سبحانه و تعالى with a guidance of a true Mukmin Guru Murshid. Zikrul Anfas has improved my understanding of why and how to perform my Solat better khusyu' inshALLAH. Zikrul Anfas truely gives me peace and tranquility in the mind and heart never before I had in my life. Once during our Ilmu trip at Pulau Besar I experienced seeing the Kalimah of ALLAH سبحانه و تعالى and Muhammad written in cloud of the high sky with 2 moons, there were a few jemaah witnessing the same thing and it indeed an amazing moment ever happened in my life. May ALLAH سبحانه و تعالى open more of my poor hijab to guide from where I have gone wrong to His Right Path inshaALLAH as I know the path is still a long way to go and yet we need to know where we need to go. This I make it known to all my dear close family inshaALLAH سبحانه و تعالى

Alhamdulillah and Praise be to ALLAH سبحانه و تعالى and blessing be to our beloved Prophet Muhammad صلى الله عليه وسلم and his Ahlul Bayt and all the Sahabahs and the

Grand Awliyas from the decendents of Sheikh Abdul Kadir Jailani RA. May ALLAH سبحانه و تعالى rewards our Guru Mursyid Sheikh Dr Ismail Kassim and his beloved family for helping and guiding me and many jemaah and his murids from all over the world with the Ilmu that ALLAH سبحانه و تعالى bestowed upon him to deliver wal dunia wal akhiroh. Amin.

Suraya Al Fakeer
The Silaturrahim/Pertubuhan Rahmatan Lil Alamin/ Halfway Home for Animals/Bela Miskin Tegar

****

Name: -Withheld-
Age: -undisclosed-
From: Selangor

بِسْمِ اللهِ الرَّحْمٰنِ الرَّحِيْمِ
اللّٰهُمَّ صَلِّ عَلَى مُحَمَّدٍ وَعَلَى آلِ مُحَمَّدٍ
فَاعْلَمْ أَنَّهُ لَا إِلٰهَ إِلَّا اللَّهُ
وتالله وبالله والله

Testimonials:

As-Salamu Alaikum.

I received bai'at zikrul anfas in 2013. I'm the type who likes to think about problems even if the matter is not so serious until I forget ALLAH سبحانه و تعالى who is the solution to all our problems. My soul is not at peace if something happens beyond my control. But alhamdulillah with zikrul anfas which was awarded by ALLAH سبحانه و تعالى and thanks to the love of Prophet Muhammad PEACE BE UPON HIM, derangement and anxiety have improved and I am more calm and leave everything to ALLAH سبحانه و تعالى to solve the problem I face. No more complications in my life and my soul and heart is quieter and always remember ALLAH سبحانه و تعالى. I always remind myself indeed this entire life belongs to ALLAH سبحانه و تعالى and only in ALLAH سبحانه و تعالى I trust. Alhamdulillah zikrul anfas have given me peace beyond words can say. I pray may ALLAH سبحانه و تعالى continue to set my heart with Kalimah لَا إِلَٰهَ إِلَّا اللَّه until my last breath.

****

Name: -Withheld-
Age: -undisclosed-
From: Selangor

بِسْمِ اللهِ الرَّحْمٰنِ الرَّحِيْمِ
اللَّهُمَّ صَلِّ عَلَى مُحَمَّدٍ وَعَلَى آلِ مُحَمَّدٍ
فَاعْلَمْ أَنَّهُ لَا إِلَٰهَ إِلَّا اللَّهُ
وتالله وبالله والله

Assalamualaikum Praise, praise to ALLAH سبحانه و تعالى, the owner of the Throne and of the universe. The highest thanks to ALLAH سبحانه و تعالى AlMighty for meeting me up with Sheikh Dr Ismail bin Kassim and his jamaah. Thanks also to Ukhtie, Kay on their invitation that I got this award.

Alhamdulillah, after getting knowledge of zikrul anfas I feel the SERENITY and PEACE of heart. My mind is calm in solving all problems of daily living. I became more grateful to continue to enjoy this life and I felt ALLAH سبحانه و تعالى THERE is ALWAYS CLOSE to me. I ALSO FEEL ALLAH سبحانه و تعالى LOVES ME.

Alhamdulillah, since I practice zikir, my heart feels light to do prayers be it wajib (obligatory) or sunat (non-obligatory). And, I am grateful most, is that ONE by ONE the miracles happens, ALLAH سبحانه و تعالى sent to settle MY DAILY LIFE PROBLEMS.

THANKS O ALLAH سبحانه و تعالى! HEARTFELT THANKS YA ALLAH سبحانه و تعالى. MY HEARTFELT THANKS TO ALL. PRAY THAT I STILL BE TOGETHER WITH JEMAAH UNTIL WE ARE IN HEAVEN.

AMIN.

****

Name : Hafizul Anuar bin Abu Bakar
Age : 36
From : Selangor

بِسْمِ اللهِ الرَّحْمٰنِ الرَّحِيْمِ
اللَّهُمَّ صَلِّ عَلَى مُحَمَّدٍ وَعَلَى آلِ مُحَمَّدٍ
فَاعْلَمْ أَنَّهُ لَا إِلٰهَ إِلَّا اللَّهُ
وتالله وبالله والله

My heart feels very contented and at peace. My mind and my spirit opens up to ALLAH سبحانه و تعالى Al Mighty.

****

Name: Abdul Malik bin Zainal Ariffin
Age:40
From: Selangor

بِسْمِ اللهِ الرَّحْمٰنِ الرَّحِيْمِ
اللَّهُمَّ صَلِّ عَلَى مُحَمَّدٍ وَعَلَى آلِ مُحَمَّدٍ
فَاعْلَمْ أَنَّهُ لَا إِلٰهَ إِلَّا اللَّهُ
وتالله وبالله والله

Alhamdulillah, I feel my heart and my mind remembers only of ALLAH سبحانه و تعالى.

****

Name: Selo Awit Abdullah
Age 34
From: Selangor

بِسْمِ اللهِ الرَّحْمٰنِ الرَّحِيْمِ
اللَّهُمَّ صَلِّ عَلَى مُحَمَّدٍ وَعَلَى آلِ مُحَمَّدٍ
فَاعْلَمْ أَنَّهُ لَا إِلٰهَ إِلَّا اللَّهُ
وتالله وبالله والله

I feel, I'm the most guilty person and the most sinful person ever. Forgive me, Ya ALLAH سبحانه و تعالى.

****

Name: Mohd Rozi
Age:50
From: -Undisclosed-

بِسْمِ اللهِ الرَّحْمٰنِ الرَّحِيْمِ
اللَّهُمَّ صَلِّ عَلَى مُحَمَّدٍ وَعَلَى آلِ مُحَمَّدٍ
فَاعْلَمْ أَنَّهُ لَا إِلٰهَ إِلَّا اللَّهُ
وتالله وبالله والله

Assalamualaikum. I can feel peace and sincerity in my prayers. I hope and pray that I get to meet Prophet Muhammad صلى الله عليه وسلم.

****

Aceh, Indonesia - Sheikh Dr Ismail Kassim
visit to Kompleks Pasentren Darussalam.

****

Name: Johan Shah bin Ibrahim
Age:29
From: Selangor

بِسْمِ اللهِ الرَّحْمنِ الرَّحِيْمِ
اللَّهُمَّ صَلِّ عَلَى مُحَمَّدٍ وَعَلَى آلِ مُحَمَّدٍ
فَاعْلَمْ أَنَّهُ لَا إِلَهَ إِلَّا اللَّهُ
وتالله وبالله والله

I can see a green coloured aura. The breathing technique
is similar to Ultra Mind Meditation.

****

Name: Mohd Faizal bin Mohd Sidek
Age:34
From: Selangor

بِسْمِ اللهِ الرَّحْمٰنِ الرَّحِيْمِ
اللَّهُمَّ صَلِّ عَلَى مُحَمَّدٍ وَعَلَى آلِ مُحَمَّدٍ
فَاعْلَمْ أَنَّهُ لَا إِلٰهَ إِلَّا اللَّهُ
وتالله وبالله والله

For me this is a very interesting program. I find that many of us knows about Kalimah لَا إِلٰهَ إِلَّا اللَّهُ but not many understands the deeper meaning and secrets of the Kalimah. This is the best program that I've ever been to and I believe this program should be expanded to all over the country for the ummah to know ALLAH سبحانه و تعالى and Prophet Muhammad ﷺ

****

Name: Mohd Wali Mohamad
Age: 35
From: Selangor

بِسْمِ اللهِ الرَّحْمٰنِ الرَّحِيْمِ
اللَّهُمَّ صَلِّ عَلَى مُحَمَّدٍ وَعَلَى آلِ مُحَمَّدٍ
فَاعْلَمْ أَنَّهُ لَا إِلٰهَ إِلَّا اللَّهُ
وتالله وبالله والله

I feel more peaceful and tranquil after the bai'at of zikrul anfas. I truly believe in this zikr.

****

Name; Mohd Nor Majnon
Age: 40
From: Selangor

بِسْمِ اللهِ الرَّحْمٰنِ الرَّحِيْمِ
اللَّهُمَّ صَلِّ عَلَى مُحَمَّدٍ وَعَلَى آلِ مُحَمَّدٍ
فَاعْلَمْ أَنَّهُ لَا إِلٰهَ إِلَّا اللَّهُ
وتالله وبالله والله

I saw the Kalimah لَا إِلٰهَ إِلَّا اللَّه for a short moment. Zikrul Anfas has a lot of benefit to us all.

****

Name: Shaharuddin Mohd Salim
Age: 39
From: Selangor

بِسْمِ اللهِ الرَّحْمٰنِ الرَّحِيْمِ
اللَّهُمَّ صَلِّ عَلَى مُحَمَّدٍ وَعَلَى آلِ مُحَمَّدٍ
فَاعْلَمْ أَنَّهُ لَا إِلٰهَ إِلَّا اللَّهُ
وتالله وبالله والله

I have received a new knowledge and received an experience that cannot be found in any religious school anywhere in this country. I now know my objective in life is to get ALLAH سبحانه و تعالى's grace and blessing. This is what I've been searching for all my life.

****

Name: Husni bin Hussin
Age:31
From: Selangor

بِسْمِ اللهِ الرَّحْمٰنِ الرَّحِيْمِ
اللَّهُمَّ صَلِّ عَلَى مُحَمَّدٍ وَعَلَى آلِ مُحَمَّدٍ
فَاعْلَمْ أَنَّهُ لَا إِلٰهَ إِلَّا اللَّهُ
وتالله وبالله والله

This is my first experience receiving zikrul anfas where I feel differences in my prayers, my manners, the way I speak and most of all my temper is now much under control.

****

Name: Risdan Sulaiman
Age:34
From:Selangor

بِسْمِ اللهِ الرَّحْمٰنِ الرَّحِيْمِ
اللَّهُمَّ صَلِّ عَلَى مُحَمَّدٍ وَعَلَى آلِ مُحَمَّدٍ
فَاعْلَمْ أَنَّهُ لَا إِلٰهَ إِلَّا اللَّهُ
وتالله وبالله والله

I was overwhelmed with emotion when I learned about zikrul anfas and started practicing it.

****

Name: Muhammad Hafizuddin
Age:22
From: Selangor

بِسْمِ اللهِ الرَّحْمٰنِ الرَّحِيْمِ
اللَّهُمَّ صَلِّ عَلَى مُحَمَّدٍ وَعَلَى آلِ مُحَمَّدٍ
فَاعْلَمْ أَنَّهُ لَا إِلٰهَ إِلَّا اللَّهُ
وتالله وبالله والله

I now understand the true meaning of لَا إِلٰهَ إِلَّا اللَّه. It enhances my faith and gives me peace. I feel very positive.

****

Name: Danny Sham
Age: 40
From: Selangor

بِسْمِ اللهِ الرَّحْمٰنِ الرَّحِيْمِ
اللَّهُمَّ صَلِّ عَلَى مُحَمَّدٍ وَعَلَى آلِ مُحَمَّدٍ
فَاعْلَمْ أَنَّهُ لَا إِلٰهَ إِلَّا اللَّهُ
وتالله وبالله والله

So much knowledge I gained from this program of zikrul anfas. I realise where my weakness are and most of all I feel peace in my heart.

****

Name: Affandi Mohd Ghouse
Age: 46
From: Selangor

بِسْمِ اللهِ الرَّحْمٰنِ الرَّحِيْمِ
اللَّهُمَّ صَلِّ عَلَى مُحَمَّدٍ وَعَلَى آلِ مُحَمَّدٍ
فَاعْلَمْ أَنَّهُ لَا إِلٰهَ إِلَّا اللَّهُ
وتالله وبالله والله

Before I attended this program, I did the zikr at home 1000 times. The face of Sheikh Ismail appeared during my zikr. I tried to forget it but image still appeared. With that sign from ALLAH سبحانه و تعالى, I came to this program to learn more about the knowledge of لَا إِلٰهَ إِلَّا اللَّه and zikrul anfas.

****

Name: Anuar Majid
Age: 44

بِسْمِ اللهِ الرَّحْمٰنِ الرَّحِيْمِ
اللَّهُمَّ صَلِّ عَلَى مُحَمَّدٍ وَعَلَى آلِ مُحَمَّدٍ
فَاعْلَمْ أَنَّهُ لَا إِلَهَ إِلَّا اللَّهُ
وتالله وبالله والله

From: I feel very peaceful and during my prayers, I could see a white aura.

****

Name: Shamir Sulaiman
Age: 24
From: Selangor

بِسْمِ اللهِ الرَّحْمٰنِ الرَّحِيْمِ
اللَّهُمَّ صَلِّ عَلَى مُحَمَّدٍ وَعَلَى آلِ مُحَمَّدٍ
فَاعْلَمْ أَنَّهُ لَا إِلَهَ إِلَّا اللَّهُ
وتالله وبالله والله

Alhamdulillah, for the most meaningful experience. I felt strong vibration throughout my body as my soul and breath gets the spiritual connection. When I prostrate to ALLAH سبحانه و تعالى, I felt the existence of ALLAH سبحانه و تعالى All Mighty.

****

Nurishah, Hyderabad, India - Walking
to a majlis program.

****

Name: Hasbullah Hussin
Age: 29
From: Selangor

بِسْمِ اللهِ الرَّحْمٰنِ الرَّحِيْم
اللَّهُمَّ صَلِّ عَلَى مُحَمَّدٍ وَعَلَى آلِ مُحَمَّدٍ
فَاعْلَمْ أَنَّهُ لَا إِلٰهَ إِلَّا اللَّهُ
وتالله وبالله والله

ALLAH سبحانه و تعالى moved me in the quest for zikrul
anfas 4 years ago. At the time my wife was very ill and
I felt the need to be closer to ALLAH سبحانه و تعالى.
Hence, I joined many tariqah groups from Naqsyabandi
to Ahmadiah and studied under many master. I was
lucky to know about this zikrul anfas program through
facebook and I immediately signed up for this program.

I feel peaceful and I could see purple and blue colour in front of my closed eyes during bai'at session.

****

Name: Nur Sabiha
Age :32
From : Selangor

بِسْمِ اللهِ الرَّحْمٰنِ الرَّحِيْمِ
اللَّهُمَّ صَلِّ عَلَى مُحَمَّدٍ وَعَلَى آلِ مُحَمَّدٍ
فَاعْلَمْ أَنَّهُ لَا إِلٰهَ إِلَّا اللَّهُ
وتالله وبالله والله

During the bai'at of zikrul anfas, my body felt very light and I felt so easy to remember ALLAH سبحانه و تعالى. It is very different previously, where my mind and focus always distracted eventhough I was in prayer.

****

Name: Fatimah Abdul Razak
Age: 35
From: Selangor

بِسْمِ اللهِ الرَّحْمٰنِ الرَّحِيْمِ
اللَّهُمَّ صَلِّ عَلَى مُحَمَّدٍ وَعَلَى آلِ مُحَمَّدٍ
فَاعْلَمْ أَنَّهُ لَا إِلٰهَ إِلَّا اللَّهُ
وتالله وبالله والله

Firstly, my experience during zikrul anfas bai'at was that I saw a white light eventhough my eyes was closed. It was like a high beam in front of my eyes and then it was gone. Secondly, I felt very emotional and I cried.

****

Name: Hazrina
Age: 45
From: Selangor

بِسْمِ اللهِ الرَّحْمٰنِ الرَّحِيْمِ
اللَّهُمَّ صَلِّ عَلَى مُحَمَّدٍ وَعَلَى آلِ مُحَمَّدٍ
فَاعْلَمْ أَنَّهُ لَا إِلٰهَ إِلَّا اللَّهُ
وتالله وبالله والله

At first, I felt a little bit confuse. Later, I felt as though I'm in Makkah. I saw Raudah, then I felt as though I was in the desert. All this happened during baiath of zikrul anfas.

****

Name: Abdul Razak
Age: 31
From: Selangor

بِسْمِ اللهِ الرَّحْمٰنِ الرَّحِيْمِ
اللَّهُمَّ صَلِّ عَلَى مُحَمَّدٍ وَعَلَى آلِ مُحَمَّدٍ

فَاعْلَمْ أَنَّهُ لَا إِلٰهَ إِلَّا اللَّهُ

وتالله وبالله والله

I felt my body shaking and vibrating during zikrul anfas bai'at. It is a feeling that cannot be described.

****

Name: Siti Rosnulawati Yunus
Age:35
From: Selangor

بِسْمِ اللهِ الرَّحْمٰنِ الرَّحِيْمِ

اللَّهُمَّ صَلِّ عَلَى مُحَمَّدٍ وَعَلَى آلِ مُحَمَّدٍ

فَاعْلَمْ أَنَّهُ لَا إِلٰهَ إِلَّا اللَّهُ

وتالله وبالله والله

During baia't, it was difficult to focus on zikr. However, slowly I felt my body vibrate, then I saw a white aura. I heard a voice telling me to continue my zikr. I was not able to stand as the vibration was too strong.

****

Name: Noorul Nadirah
Age: 28
From: Selangor

بِسْمِ اللهِ الرَّحْمٰنِ الرَّحِيْمِ
اللَّهُمَّ صَلِّ عَلَى مُحَمَّدٍ وَعَلَى آلِ مُحَمَّدٍ
فَاعْلَمْ أَنَّهُ لَا إِلٰهَ إِلَّا اللّٰهُ
وتالله وبالله والله

During my zikrul anfas training, I tried to denounce my existence and relate that only ALLAH سبحانه و تعالى exist. I then felt my heart beating with the kalimah ALLAH سبحانه و تعالى. I could not move, my body froze, from there I understood the meaning of Lahaulawalaquwataillabillah. ALLAH سبحانه و تعالى please open the veils that hides you.

****

Name: Hazrul bin Ahmad
Age: 32
From: Selangor

بِسْمِ اللهِ الرَّحْمٰنِ الرَّحِيْمِ
اللَّهُمَّ صَلِّ عَلَى مُحَمَّدٍ وَعَلَى آلِ مُحَمَّدٍ
فَاعْلَمْ أَنَّهُ لَا إِلٰهَ إِلَّا اللّٰهُ
وتالله وبالله والله

Alhamdulillah, I'm so thankful to ALLAH سبحانه و تعالى for the blessing of zikrul anfas to me. This is the highest gift from ALLAH سبحانه و تعالى a person can get for all his life here on earth. I feel very contented and focus of the objective in this life in learning the knowledge of لَا إِلَٰهَ إِلَّا اللَّه, knowledge of syahadah, knowledge of true faith and iman.

****

Name: Muhammad Azrul Abdul Aziz
Age: 31
From: Selangor

بِسْمِ اللهِ الرَّحْمٰنِ الرَّحِيْمِ
اللَّهُمَّ صَلِّ عَلَى مُحَمَّدٍ وَعَلَى آلِ مُحَمَّدٍ
فَاعْلَمْ أَنَّهُ لَا إِلَٰهَ إِلَّا اللَّهُ
وتالله وبالله والله

Alhamdulillah, before I received the zikrul anfas, my breath zikr was always not consistent and stuttering. Now, with having zikrul anfas my breath zikr becomes smooth. My prayers are more focused and disturbance in prayers are less.

****

Name : Zainul Anuar
Age: 48
From : Negeri Sembilan

بِسْمِ اللهِ الرَّحْمٰنِ الرَّحِيْمِ
اللَّهُمَّ صَلِّ عَلَى مُحَمَّدٍ وَعَلَى آلِ مُحَمَّدٍ

فَاعْلَمْ أَنَّهُ لَا إِلَٰهَ إِلَّا اللَّهُ

وتالله وبالله والله

After receiving zikrul anfas my life is more stable. My business improved and got better. I'm able to focus on learning the Kalimah لَا إِلَٰهَ إِلَّا اللَّهُ with the extra time that I have as my business is now under control.

****

Name: Mohd Yasir

Age: 30

From: Selangor

بِسْمِ اللهِ الرَّحْمٰنِ الرَّحِيْمِ

اللَّهُمَّ صَلِّ عَلَى مُحَمَّدٍ وَعَلَى آلِ مُحَمَّدٍ

فَاعْلَمْ أَنَّهُ لَا إِلَٰهَ إِلَّا اللَّهُ

وتالله وبالله والله

Feels as though, I've been born again. The highest gift from ALLAH سبحانه و تعالى when I received the zikrul anfas. Alhamdulillah, feels relaxed, comfortable, peaceful and focused in my prayers.

****

Abdul Rahman bin Abdul Rahim

Age : 32

From: Selangor

بِسْمِ اللهِ الرَّحْمٰنِ الرَّحِيْمِ
اللَّهُمَّ صَلِّ عَلَى مُحَمَّدٍ وَعَلَى آلِ مُحَمَّدٍ
فَاعْلَمْ أَنَّهُ لَا إِلٰهَ إِلَّا اللَّهُ
وتالله وبالله والله

Alhamdulillah, syukran to ALLAH سبحانه و تعالى for his blessings of zikrul anfas. I feel the tranquility, contentment as though I've just been born. May ALLAH سبحانه و تعالى keep us in this path until we return back to him.

****

Name: Firdaus bin Amat
Age: 35
From: Selangor

بِسْمِ اللهِ الرَّحْمٰنِ الرَّحِيْمِ
اللَّهُمَّ صَلِّ عَلَى مُحَمَّدٍ وَعَلَى آلِ مُحَمَّدٍ
فَاعْلَمْ أَنَّهُ لَا إِلٰهَ إِلَّا اللَّهُ
وتالله وبالله والله

Alhamdulillah, eversince bestowed with zikrul anfas, I feel very contented and tranquil. My breath feels as if it is filled with energy, such a pleasure.

****

Name: Roslan bin Mohd
Age: 51
From: Selangor

بِسْمِ اللهِ الرَّحْمٰنِ الرَّحِيْمِ
اللَّهُمَّ صَلِّ عَلَى مُحَمَّدٍ وَعَلَى آلِ مُحَمَّدٍ
فَاعْلَمْ أَنَّهُ لَا إِلٰهَ إِلَّا اللَّهُ
وتالله وبالله والله

I am so thankful to ALLAH سبحانه و تعالى, that after 3 sessions of joining the magnet nafas and magnet syahadah program, I was bestowed with zikrul anfas. InsyaALLAH سبحانه و تعالى, I will adhere to all the rules and adab in learning knowledge of Kalimah لَا إِلٰهَ إِلَّا اللَّهُ.

****

Name: Muhammad Irsyad bin Roslan
Age : 19
From: Selangor

بِسْمِ اللهِ الرَّحْمٰنِ الرَّحِيْمِ
اللَّهُمَّ صَلِّ عَلَى مُحَمَّدٍ وَعَلَى آلِ مُحَمَّدٍ
فَاعْلَمْ أَنَّهُ لَا إِلٰهَ إِلَّا اللَّهُ
وتالله وبالله والله

I'm so thankful to ALLAH سبحانه و تعالى for this precious gift of zikrul anfas. I am very confident in

learning the knowledge of LaailahaillALLAH سبحانه و
تعالى.

****

Name: Muhammad Mukhriz bin Roslan
Age: 21
From: Selangor

بِسْمِ اللهِ الرَّحْمٰنِ الرَّحِيْمِ
اللَّهُمَّ صَلِّ عَلَى مُحَمَّدٍ وَعَلَى آلِ مُحَمَّدٍ
فَاعْلَمْ أَنَّهُ لَا إِلٰهَ إِلَّا اللَّهُ
وتالله وبالله والله

Alhamdulillah, ever since I started to do regular zikrul anfas breathing, my heart feels so contented and all my problems have been removed and destroyed. لَا إِلٰهَ إِلَّا اللَّهُ is the knowledge that must be learned by all muslims.

****

Name: Alias Hamdi
Age : 34
From: Selangor

بِسْمِ اللهِ الرَّحْمٰنِ الرَّحِيْمِ
اللَّهُمَّ صَلِّ عَلَى مُحَمَّدٍ وَعَلَى آلِ مُحَمَّدٍ
فَاعْلَمْ أَنَّهُ لَا إِلٰهَ إِلَّا اللَّهُ
وتالله وبالله والله

After I took zikrul anfas I felt inner peace in my soul. My parents and siblings all was bestowed with zikrul anfas. Our life have become more focused and we strive to share this knowledge with all our muslim brothers so that they too can become mukmins and feel the spiritual blessings.

****

****

Name: Mohd Yazid
Age: -undisclosed-
From: Selangor

بِسْمِ اللهِ الرَّحْمٰنِ الرَّحِيْمِ
اللَّهُمَّ صَلِّ عَلَى مُحَمَّدٍ وَعَلَى آلِ مُحَمَّدٍ
فَاعْلَمْ أَنَّهُ لَا إِلٰهَ إِلَّا اللَّهُ
وتالله وبالله والله

Testimonials:

Here's my Experience

BAIAH ZIKRUL ANFAS : 12th DECEMBER 2013

Here's my Experience

Alhamdulilah, Syukur to ALLAH سبحانه و تعالى and Salawat to Muhammad Rasulullah Habibullah ﷺ. Some spiritual experience of spirituality since receiving zikrul anfas, including:

1. Often remember in the heart in zikrullah (ALLAH سبحانه و تعالى Hu ALLAH سبحانه و تعالى, ALLAH سبحانه و تعالى ALLAH سبحانه و تعالى, Lailaha IlALLAH سبحانه و تعالى, Hu Hu and others

2. Training and practice zikrul anfas every day strengthens focus & feels healthier

3. During the program in Acheh, many spiritual experiences felt when the program of zikir and selawat as well as visiting the residence of the aulia, one of the significant things I felt was, the presence of Nur in my heart.

4. Experience in Acheh is also experience of the heart. My heart feels very emotional and often crying, when salawat being read, when Prophet's name mentioned, when Sheikh Abdul Qadir Jilani name mentioned and when hugging

Honorable Sheikh Dr Ismail and when I hug orphaned children.

5. Feeling of love to Prophet ﷺ and increase salawat to him.

6. Felt the presence of nur during zikr makes the whole body chanting, swaying because of the exciting voice of zikr followed by a hard and strong voice.

This is some of the experience I have experience thus far. I pray for doa from Sheikh so that I will stay on this path and increase my faith constantly in order to reach HAQ ALLAH سبحانه و تعالى.

I am so thankful to ALLAH سبحانه و تعالى for meeting me up with a mursyid who never fails to guide and provide Light, wisdom to the path of siratul mustaqeem.

JazakALLAHu khairan kasira.

****

Name: Taufiq Yahya
Age: 31 Years
From: Kuala Lumpur

بِسْمِ اللهِ الرَّحْمٰنِ الرَّحِيْمِ
اللَّهُمَّ صَلِّ عَلَى مُحَمَّدٍ وَعَلَى آلِ مُحَمَّدٍ
فَاعْلَمْ أَنَّهُ لَا إِلَٰهَ إِلَّا اللَّهُ
وتالله وبالله والله

89

Testimonials:

My life in the past was very problematic; as there were no encouragement and always feeling of despair over life's matter such as finance, debt and employment. I also always blame others for my problems. Often the feeling of stress is too great that I feel like dying; but strange I never felt the fear of sin, nor fear the tribulation in the grave and the torment of hell even though I know that ALLAH سبحانه و تعالى is true. I often look for entertainment outside until late morning to quieten my soul but still I didn't get the peace. All worship becomes very heavy to do, especially, the 5 times solat prayers. When performing solat, there is no focus. I always forget my Raka'ats. The Qur'an has never been read for many years, despite attending religious boarding school while growing up. Alhamdulillah, thanks to the prayers and guidance of my parents, my wife and family members as well as my Masyaikh. Ever since Ramadan 2011, I started to follow the majlis and knowledge by Sheikh Dr Ismail Kassim. Gratitude for the blessings of faith of لا إله إلا الله محمد رسول الله ﷺ on my second visit to Pulau Besar, Malacca, during Ramadan 2013, ALLAH سبحانه و تعالى gifted me with zikrul anfas.

My heart and feelings were very quiet and calm since I received and practiced zikrul anfas, even though life's problem was still a lot. Temperament is also not easily upset and I'm able to control my emotions more easily. Performing worship feels lighter and full of appreciation, and when I read the Quran and zikrullah, I'm overwhelmed and touched and tends to cry. Income is getting better as well as working life has improved and there is an increase of sales to thousands of ringgit each month; until now Alhamdulillah everything ALLAH سبحانه و تعالى is giving all enough for me.

My diabetes problem has improved. Since 2010 my diabetes is not properly cared and uncontrolled, now it is under control. Alhamdulillah I am confident if we go after ALLAH سبحانه و تعالى in this world and returned the breath and everything to him, ALLAH و سبحانه تعالى will make the world come to us. Wallaahu a'lam

****

Name: -Withheld-
Age: 30 Years
From: Malacca

بِسْمِ اللهِ الرَّحْمٰنِ الرَّحِيْمِ
اللَّهُمَّ صَلِّ عَلَى مُحَمَّدٍ وَعَلَى آلِ مُحَمَّدٍ
فَاعْلَمْ أَنَّهُ لَا إِلٰهَ إِلَّا اللَّهُ
وتالله وبالله والله

Testimonials:

Praise and Gratitude to ALLAH سبحانه و تعالى. To be chosen to receive a great gift that is zikrul anfas. First and foremost, during the talqeen of zikrul anfas I felt very calm and felt as though I was in another realm. After receiving zikrul anfas, while I am asleep I dreamt I was making zikr. I had experienced this numerous times. Alhamdulillah, I have never felt such experience before receiving zikrul anfas. My everyday life have changed a lot, I always remember ALLAH سبحانه و تعالى, even when I forget, I will automatically remember again. At that time I will naturally repent to ALLAH سبحانه و تعالى.

Alhamdulillah, Thank you O ALLAH سبحانه و تعالى for choosing me, who is dirty and full of sin to receive this precious gift.

****

Name: Khairul
Age: -undisclosed
From: Kuala Lumpur

بِسْمِ اللهِ الرَّحْمٰنِ الرَّحِيْمِ
اللَّهُمَّ صَلِّ عَلَى مُحَمَّدٍ وَعَلَى آلِ مُحَمَّدٍ
فَاعْلَمْ أَنَّهُ لَا إِلٰهَ إِلَّا اللَّهُ
وتالله وبالله والله

Testimonials:

Bismillahirahmanirahim, in the name of ALLAH سبحانه و تعالى, most gracious, most merciful.

Alhamdulillah with the practice of the kalimah of zikrul anfas by the teaching Honorable Sheikh Dr Ismail Kassim. Directly and indirectly it has already absorbed as a cultural-like practice for myself every day.

Through zikrul anfas it can be seen of the many changes to myself.

First – my life and my self is always calm and I am clean from transgressions.

Second - Blessings of life and always remembering ALLAH سبحانه و تعالى.

Third - ALLAH سبحانه و تعالى eases most affairs and personal safety.

Fourth - All the knowledge of dunia and akhirah learnt is easy to be remembered and practiced.

Fifth – Always patient and self-reminding

Sixth - Loving humans and animals.

Seventh - Loving environment.

****

Name: -Withheld
Age: -undisclosed
From: Selangor

بِسْمِ اللهِ الرَّحْمٰنِ الرَّحِيْمِ
اللَّهُمَّ صَلِّ عَلَى مُحَمَّدٍ وَعَلَى آلِ مُحَمَّدٍ
فَاعْلَمْ أَنَّهُ لَا إِلٰهَ إِلَّا اللَّهُ
وتالله وبالله والله

Testimonials:

Assalamualaikum. I would like to express here my experience before and after the bai'at of zikrul anfas. Before I joined PERAHMAT, my life was full of stress, outside and within myself. After meeting and joining the group PERAHMAT, I feel more relaxed and rich with love. I am not saying that I have never felt like this before, it is just that now everything has become more beautiful and graceful.

My life now comprises of many challenges, tests and obstacle. There will always be something in the way and be of a challenge to my life. However, with the teaching of Honorable Sheikh Dr Ismail Kassim and with the knowledge I have learned, it embellishes my life and in my heart to be grateful to ALLAH سبحانه و تعالى. I've become truly patient and confident in any distress that comes my way now. Regardless at times of sadness or triumph, by praying and remembering ALLAH سبحانه

تعالى و, my life now full of meaning and intention to understand the knowledge of ALLAH سبحانه و تعالى.

EVERYTHING FOR ALLAH سبحانه و تعالى, INSYAALLAH, AMIN.

****

Name: Ismail Bin Sabudin
Age: -undisclosed
From: KLIA, Sepang, Selangor

بِسْمِ اللهِ الرَّحْمٰنِ الرَّحِيْمِ
اللَّهُمَّ صَلِّ عَلَى مُحَمَّدٍ وَعَلَى آلِ مُحَمَّدٍ
فَاعْلَمْ أَنَّهُ لَا إِلٰهَ إِلَّا اللَّهُ
وتالله وبالله والله

Testimonials: When being talqin with zikrul anfas by Sheikh Dr Ismail Kassim, I can feel a calmness in my soul. I cry incessantly during bai'at. Crying is not fake, but the tears flow because the heart feels near to the divine light of truth. One thing that I feel while being talqin with the zikrul anfas is I can feel as if my ruh or soul on the move and fly by so fast. I can't control myself to stop. Alhamdulillah, this is a true knowledge.

From: South Malaysia

Name: Badrul Mohamed
Age: 44 Years
From: Ulu Tiram, Johor

بِسْمِ اللهِ الرَّحْمٰنِ الرَّحِيْمِ
اللَّهُمَّ صَلِّ عَلَى مُحَمَّدٍ وَعَلَى آلِ مُحَمَّدٍ
فَاعْلَمْ أَنَّهُ لَا إِلَهَ إِلَّا اللَّهُ
وتالله وبالله والله

Testimonials: Date of talqeen: 16/11/2013.

Experience during talqIn of the Zikrul Anfas.

1. I felt my breath move in and out continuously and moving as if a "vertical tawaf" and the breath moves in an out again by itself.
2. My whole body felt cold.
3. I felt like being inside myself.

Zikrul Anfas and the peaceful mind.

1. If something happens or when I'm dealing with something, my mind will be more calm facing these situations and my heart will refer to Qada, Qadar, Qudrat and His Iradat.
2. When learning the knowledge of kalimah, I can see the connections between sight and an event is from the Af'al of ALLAH سبحانه و تعالى.
3. When I do tafakur I could focus more deeply on the power and magnificence of ALLAH سبحانه و تعالى to the whole universe to the smallest of atoms
4. My heart became more sensitive and I feel touched towards anything relating to love of Rasulullah ﷺ and his Companions.
5. I could learn to control my views and feelings from things that are bad.

Zikrul Anfas and Khusyu' of Prayers.

1. By learning the knowledge of Kalimah I could better understand the verses that is being recited.

2. I feel less of my mind and heart drifting away in prayers.

3. While I am yet to reach the level of khusyu, the depth, the entireness and flawlessness of prayer and syahadah but I was able to learn to syahadah and feel to the attributes of ALLAH سبحانه و تعالى in my prayers such as the Attributes of Qudrat, Iradat, Ilm, Hayat, Sama', Basyar and Kalam.

4. When I have a slight disturbance in my prayers, it felt like I was watched and close to ALLAH سبحانه و تعالى.

****

Name: **Withheld**
Age: -undisclosed-
From: Johor

بِسْمِ اللهِ الرَّحْمٰنِ الرَّحِيْمِ
اللَّهُمَّ صَلِّ عَلَى مُحَمَّدٍ وَعَلَى آلِ مُحَمَّدٍ
فَاعْلَمْ أَنَّهُ لَا إِلٰهَ إِلَّا اللَّهُ
وتالله وبالله والله

Testimonials: Alhamdu lilahi rabbilalamin, wassolahtu wa Rasullilahi wa salamu'alaika 'ala alihi wa sohbihi wa salam.

I was introduced to Honorable Sheikh Dr Ismail Kassim in 2012 in Melaka. After attending the majlis at Pulau

Besar, I received zikr anfas through Sheikh Dr Ismail Kassim, 1434 Hijiriah at 21 Rajab.

Alhamdulillah, let me share my experience. Zikrul anfas is the gift from ALLAH سبحانه و تعالى to the believer, who is always on the path to find ALLAH سبحانه و تعالى in his heart. Firman ALLAH سبحانه و تعالى surah Azzukhruf verse 36:

Whoever turned away from Arrahman, we will make the devil to befriend and join them. It is the responsibility of every muslim to become a believer, from not knowing, to knowing, from confusion to comprehension, from questions to answers, we have to apply from Rabbul Alamin 'to give light to aqal, qalbu, spirit also to the sirr. So zikrul anfas is the best gift from ALLAH سبحانه و تعالى as a medium in the remembrance of ALLAH سبحانه و تعالى. If we do not have this zikrul anfas we belong among the evil-doers.

Zikrul anfas can calm and give focus during prayers. Previously it was very difficult for me to focus during prayers. In our daily work, previously I felt pressured by the burden of daily work, Remembrance of ALLAH Hu ALAH and zikrul anfas helps me get a peace of mind. In addition, the love for the Prophet (PBUH) also increased, and be part of his jihad. All acts and incidents I see it all from ALLAH سبحانه و تعالى's Afaal, as well as to increase the understanding of the Syahadah at the time of remembrance. La hawla wa la quwwata ila billah, the feeling of this self has no power, qudrat, iradah everything without the consent and power of ALLAH سبحانه و تعالى. I also feel so little to ALLAH سبحانه و تعالى and powerless unless given by ALLAH سبحانه و تعالى to do something. At the same time being able to practice and improve understanding of tauhidul afaal, tauhidul asma, tauhidus jasad and tauhiduz zat.

Also I can feel, my fight with my nafs such as bad temper, arrogance which I try to subdue. Little by little, I'm able to destroy the nafs' chains with zikr anfas. With ALLAH سبحانه و تعالى's consent and learning of the knowledge of syahadah by Sheikh Dr Ismail Kassim, I can feel faith, confidence, submission, tawakkal and zikrullah. Thanks to the grace of ALLAH سبحانه و تعالى as guide, teacher and bring us to his love. Thank you for letting me share my experience after receiving the zikrul anfas.

Salam and Al Fatihah to Sayidul Mursalin, Rasulillahi صلى الله عليه وسلم, his family, his friends,

Masyaikh, Shaykh Gauts Al A'zam Sheikh Abdul Qadir Gilani QSA.

****

Aceh. Indonesia – Sheikh Dr Ismail
Kassim Visit To Sabang Island

From: Singapore

Name: Abdul Razak
Age: -undisclosed-
From: Singapore

بِسْمِ اللهِ الرَّحْمٰنِ الرَّحِيْمِ
اللَّهُمَّ صَلِّ عَلَى مُحَمَّدٍ وَعَلَى آلِ مُحَمَّدٍ
فَاعْلَمْ أَنَّهُ لَا إِلٰهَ إِلَّا اللَّهُ
وتالله وبالله والله

As salamu Alaikum Sheik. Bismilahirahmanir Rahim

Let me introduce myself. My name is Abdul Razak Bin Abdul Kader. I am 48 years old living in Singapore. Am married with 4 siblings. I received the baiyah from Sheik Muhibishah رضي الله عنه (a murshid from Silsilah Chistia Qadaria Tarika). My sheik's grand sheik is from Hyderbad Sheik Noorisha Kibla رضي الله عنه. Throughout this period and when my sheik visit us in Singapore. Daily we attend his classes on Kalima لا إله إلا الله. Although with the blessings of the silsilah I do managed to understand the Kalima bits and pieces but I still did not receive the full spectrum of the Kalima.

Thereafter, my Sarga left after few weeks. We had also followed him to Johor and Penang. He left for India after spending a few weeks. This happened sometime in 1988-89.

There was always burning desire in me to know ALLAH سبحانه و تعالى and to be with ALLAH سبحانه و تعالى. Till then my desire to know the Kalimah Syahadah was accumulating and fuming in my heart day by day till the day I saw your youtube speech. I was asking ALLAH سبحانه و تعالى to show me a mursyid where I can continue the learning and know the intrepretation of the Kalimah Syahadah until I saw u and your speech which errupted me further. Indeed the Kalimah Syahadah on the mubtiloon had shaken me.

I am immensely attracted by your great speech (that came from ALLAH سبحانه و تعالى rabul izzat without doubt). Your speech has reactivated my Zikrul Anfas and I have immediately started to see and practice the Syahadah daily. I would very much like to receive your "thithar"(chance to meet u). If you wish and permit please let me know if I can attend your majlis Insha ALLAH سبحانه و تعالى.

Sheikh I have short comings and has made great mistakes in life. I am asking for ALLAH سبحانه و تعالى to forgive my sins. Please also doa for me and my family to ALLAH سبحانه و تعالى to wipe me and my family sins and receive the blessings of Prophet Muhammad Rasulullah ﷺ. Ameen.

****

Name: Syed Abdul Aziz
Age: 40
From: Singapore

بِسْمِ اللهِ الرَّحْمٰنِ الرَّحِيْمِ

اللَّهُمَّ صَلِّ عَلَى مُحَمَّدٍ وَعَلَى آلِ مُحَمَّدٍ

فَاعْلَمْ أَنَّهُ لَا إِلَٰهَ إِلَّا اللَّهُ
وتالله وبالله والله

My Zikrul Anfas Experience

Syukur Alhamdulilah out of billions of people on this planet earth, and zillions of other creatures of ALLAH سبحانه و تعالى, visible or invisible on this planet and beyond. There are a few people fated to receive the zikir nafas on Pulau Besar Melaka.

The experience that I had was that I used to hear all these "voices" that encourage me to do things which I know was wrong but end up doing it. Sheikh Dr Ismail Haji Kassim gave me the zikrul anfas. All these voices became quiet, I was really enjoying the silence and peace. So these voices do come back once in a while, but there is always another voice that reminds to bring me back and do the right thing. Zikrul Anfas is not only a heart purification through ALLAH سبحانه و تعالى's remembrance but also a supreme invisible shield and weapon against the enemies within.

Post Zikrul Anfas experience.

On the way home, I start to witness that my prayers are heard. It is things that I used to take for granted. I felt calm and I felt that ALLAH سبحانه و تعالى is always close to me. Was rushing for the ferry, and afraid that I might miss the bus, but all went smooth. Every step of the way, I felt calm and not worried at all about anything.

Even though when I arrived at the ferry terminal, there was no taxi but just a whisper in the heart and ALLAH سبحانه و تعالى opens the way for me. The timings were just perfect and the calmness of having to know of HIS presence and his power is amazing!

I became thirsty, thirsty for knowledge. I drives me to seek it, I spend sometime "dating" with ALLAH سبحانه و تعالى after my sholat. Just sitting down on the sejadah and have a heart to heart talk with ALLAH سبحانه و تعالى. I know there is nothing in the heart that could be hidden that ALLAH سبحانه و تعالى does not know.

I opened up to HIM, prayed to Him for forgiveness and pray to him not to let me die kufur. To improve oneself is to know oneself, and to know the enemy for our internal Jihad. Which is the greatest battle for Mankind. I need HIS help and His guidance, and to get that help the key thing Is Remembrance = Zikrul Anfas and Surrender to Almighty ALLAH سبحانه و تعالى what He wills me to be. Find a Mursyid who has links to Our Holy Beloved Prophet Muhammad Rasulullah ﷺ who will guide us. Then we are on the Right Path. Insya-ALLAH سبحانه و تعالى.

****

Aceh. Indonesia – Sheikh Dr Ismail Kassim Lecture
At Prasentren Darussalam Labohan Haji

From: East Malaysia

Name: **Mohd Yusof Bin Hamdi**
Age: -undisclosed-
From: Kota Kinabalu

بِسْمِ اللهِ الرَّحْمٰنِ الرَّحِيْمِ

اللَّهُمَّ صَلِّ عَلَى مُحَمَّدٍ وَعَلَى آلِ مُحَمَّدٍ

فَاعْلَمْ أَنَّهُ لَا إِلٰهَ إِلَّا اللَّهُ

وتالله وبالله والله

Testimonials: My soul feels at peace after receiving zikrul anfas from Honorable Sheikh Dr Ismail Kassim.

I'm very confident and believe that this is the highest knowledge to ALLAH سبحانه و تعالى.

I get to know the whispers of our enemy, nafs and satan who always trying to deviate me. But now, armed with this zikrul anfas, I can beat nafs and satan easily.

There is a moment where I was sitting and doing zikrul anfas and then I felt as if I was in a place like in the forest. It was quiet and lonely, and so quiet and I could only hear the sound of birds – birds ... Truly amazing.

This is how I see my life right now; I've got keys to the right car, and this car can start and move because the key matches with the car. Alhamdulillah. Now I am on the right and true path. Previously, in the past, I've got the key but the key cannot be used to start the car.

****

Name: Mohd Naim
Age: -undisclosed-
From: Kota Kinabalu

بِسْمِ اللهِ الرَّحْمٰنِ الرَّحِيْمِ
اللَّهُمَّ صَلِّ عَلَى مُحَمَّدٍ وَعَلَى آلِ مُحَمَّدٍ
فَاعْلَمْ أَنَّهُ لَا إِلٰهَ إِلَّا اللَّهُ
وتالله وبالله والله

Testimonials: I felt happy and quiet while I was taking bai'at of zikrul anfas from Honorable Sheikh Dr Ismail Kassim. When I got the zikrul anfas, I felt I was high in space and I see a green coloured light on both my right and left side.

Now I often dream about spiritual things such as I saw a mosque with no one in it, then I go in and pray alone. There is also a dream that I see the arabic alphabets -mim, ba, ya and ra.

Alhamdulillah, my life feel so meaningful now.

****

Name: **Ramdan Samudin**
Age: -undisclosed-
From: Kota Kinabalu

بِسْمِ اللهِ الرَّحْمٰنِ الرَّحِيْمِ
اللَّهُمَّ صَلِّ عَلَى مُحَمَّدٍ وَعَلَى آلِ مُحَمَّدٍ
فَاعْلَمْ أَنَّهُ لَا إِلٰهَ إِلَّا اللَّهُ
وتالله وبالله والله

Testimonials: I remembered when I was being talqin with the zikrul anfas by Honorable Sheikh Dr Ismail Kassim, I feel so peaceful. At the time of the talqin, I felt so sleepy and some sort like sleeping, but actually, I was ceaselessly doing zikir لا إله إلا الله and when I came to my senses, I find myself in the position of the Tahyat akhir of the prayers.

There is one event after the talqin of zikrul anfas, where I visited a friend where his brother was disturbed by genie. At that time there were a few Ustaz attending to the brother and was using rukyah to drive off the genie out of the brother's body. But the genie still did not want to come out from the brother's body, at the same time I reached to my friends home for my visit.

Suddenly, at that time, the genie ran out of the brother's body, to a boy who was also in the house. The genie than said through the boy, to Ustaz, that he was scared of me because I've got a secret that no other people have and the secret brings very strong light. I realized and thought that the secrets that I bring is no other than the zikrul anfas of ALLAH Hu ALLAH. Alhamdulillah. This is one of the most precious gift from ALLAH سبحانه و تعالى. Wasallam.

****

Name: **Herorio Bin Awang**
Age: -undisclosed-
From: Sandakan

بِسْمِ اللهِ الرَّحْمٰنِ الرَّحِيْمِ
اللَّهُمَّ صَلِّ عَلَى مُحَمَّدٍ وَعَلَى آلِ مُحَمَّدٍ

فَاعْلَمْ أَنَّهُ لَا إِلَهَ إِلَّا اللَّهُ

وتالله وبالله والله

Testimonials: Changes to self: After getting zikrul anfas I receive peace-filled mind and heart which is difficult to obtain anywhere else. When I hear the Azan, I feel very happy and easy to do solat. Dream: Met an old man with cane.

****

Name: **Hirmanto**

Age: -undisclosed-

From: Sandakan

بِسْمِ اللهِ الرَّحْمَنِ الرَّحِيْمِ

اللَّهُمَّ صَلِّ عَلَى مُحَمَّدٍ وَعَلَى آلِ مُحَمَّدٍ

فَاعْلَمْ أَنَّهُ لَا إِلَهَ إِلَّا اللَّهُ

وتالله وبالله والله

Testimonials: Changes to self: Always quiet and resilient when receiving ALLAH سبحانه و تعالى's tests, I feel very patient when tested. Wake up early than usual for subuh prayer.

Dreams: I saw my deceased teacher making a drain near his house.

****

Name: **Mohd Hafiez Bin Mat Husni**
Age: -undisclosed-
From: Sandakan

بِسْمِ اللهِ الرَّحْمٰنِ الرَّحِيْمِ
اللَّهُمَّ صَلِّ عَلَى مُحَمَّدٍ وَعَلَى آلِ مُحَمَّدٍ
فَاعْلَمْ أَنَّهُ لَا إِلَهَ إِلَّا اللَّهُ
وتالله وبالله والله

Testimonials: Changes to self : more accepting of the test received from ALLAH سبحانه و تعالى. I can feel the sweetness of making prayer and other amal to a point where I do not want to stop making zikr and salawat to Rasul'ALLAH ﷺ. Sustenance from ALLAH سبحانه و تعالى is added without realizing and comfortable with people around.

Dreams of brother Fairul reminding me not to forget doing zikrul anfas.

****

Name: Mohammed Sarji Bin Hussein
Age: -undisclosed-
From: Sandakan

بِسْمِ اللهِ الرَّحْمٰنِ الرَّحِيْمِ
اللَّهُمَّ صَلِّ عَلَى مُحَمَّدٍ وَعَلَى آلِ مُحَمَّدٍ
فَاعْلَمْ أَنَّهُ لَا إِلَهَ إِلَّا اللَّهُ
وتالله وبالله والله

Testimonials: I have been searching for a long time for knowledge that could bring me to the divine One. I feel peace when I was talqined with the zikrul anfas.

****

Name: Mohsin Bin Jurop
Age: -undisclosed-
From: Sandakan

بِسْمِ اللهِ الرَّحْمٰنِ الرَّحِيْمِ

اللّٰهُمَّ صَلِّ عَلٰى مُحَمَّدٍ وَعَلٰى آلِ مُحَمَّدٍ

فَاعْلَمْ أَنَّهُ لَا إِلٰهَ إِلَّا اللّٰهُ

وتالله وبالله والله

Testimonials: I felt a calm and peaceful while being talqin with the zikrul anfas by Mursyid Sheikh Dr Ismail Kassim. I still feel peace of mind until today. One thing that is very obvious after getting zikrul anfas is my temper has much decreased. In fact I am more patient in facing the challenges and problems surrounding me at work, even at home. Wasallam.

From: Aceh, Indonesia

Nur Azizah
Age: 45 years

بِسْمِ اللهِ الرَّحْمٰنِ الرَّحِيْمِ
اللَّهُمَّ صَلِّ عَلَى مُحَمَّدٍ وَعَلَى آلِ مُحَمَّدٍ
فَاعْلَمْ أَنَّهُ لَا إِلٰهَ إِلَّا اللَّهُ
وتالله وبالله والله

Testimonial: Alhamdulillah, after receiving the zikrul anfas. My heart feels tranquil, peace and happy, closer to ALLAH سبحانه و تعالى. My heart wants to always be in zikr and to learn Kalimah لا إله إلا الله. For me, zikr of the breath is a blessing of utmost high value, in my

115

journey towards ALLAH سبحانه و تعالى (just to gain love and compassion of ALLAH سبحانه و تعالى Almighty).

****

Name: Suriati Binti Abdul Halim
Age: 35 years

بِسْمِ اللهِ الرَّحْمٰنِ الرَّحِيْمِ
اللّٰهُمَّ صَلِّ عَلَى مُحَمَّدٍ وَعَلَى آلِ مُحَمَّدٍ
فَاعْلَمْ أَنَّهُ لَا إِلٰهَ إِلَّا اللَّهُ
وتالله وبالله والله

Testimonial: Calm, happy and Overwhelmed.

****

Name: Nurjannah Binti M. Nur
Age: 38 years

بِسْمِ اللهِ الرَّحْمٰنِ الرَّحِيْمِ
اللّٰهُمَّ صَلِّ عَلَى مُحَمَّدٍ وَعَلَى آلِ مُحَمَّدٍ
فَاعْلَمْ أَنَّهُ لَا إِلٰهَ إِلَّا اللَّهُ
وتالله وبالله والله

Testimonial: Feel happy, sad, released from all burden. I saw colors, purple and green.

Name: Marliana Binti Sumarlin Saragih

Age: 26 years

بِسْمِ اللهِ الرَّحْمٰنِ الرَّحِيْمِ

اللَّهُمَّ صَلِّ عَلَى مُحَمَّدٍ وَعَلَى آلِ مُحَمَّدٍ

فَاعْلَمْ أَنَّهُ لَا إِلَهَ إِلَّا اللَّهُ

وتالله وبالله والله

Testimonial: Alhamdulillah after receiving bai'at zikrul anfas, I feel calm and the burden I carry feels lighter. Prior to doing zikr, I had a dream, where next to the hostel there is a teacher, who greeted me and I then ran to my room for fear. After my prayers, somebody pat my shoulder and said "don't be afraid". The Sheikh looks like Sheikh Dr Ismail bin Kassim.

****

Name: Muhammad Ridha Bin M. Nur

Age: 33 years

بِسْمِ اللهِ الرَّحْمٰنِ الرَّحِيْمِ

اللَّهُمَّ صَلِّ عَلَى مُحَمَّدٍ وَعَلَى آلِ مُحَمَّدٍ

فَاعْلَمْ أَنَّهُ لَا إِلَهَ إِلَّا اللَّهُ

وتالله وبالله والله

Testimonials: Feel calm, Peaceful and happy.
Name: Jumadil Firdaus Bin M. Nur
Age: 29 years

بِسْمِ اللهِ الرَّحْمٰنِ الرَّحِيْمِ
اللَّهُمَّ صَلِّ عَلَى مُحَمَّدٍ وَعَلَى آلِ مُحَمَّدٍ
فَاعْلَمْ أَنَّهُ لَا إِلٰهَ إِلَّا اللَّهُ
وتالله وبالله والله

Testimonials: Feel calm, happy, hearts want to always zikr, feel more patient.

****

Name: Kaifal Bin Muhammad Amin
Age: 19 years

بِسْمِ اللهِ الرَّحْمٰنِ الرَّحِيْمِ
اللَّهُمَّ صَلِّ عَلَى مُحَمَّدٍ وَعَلَى آلِ مُحَمَّدٍ
فَاعْلَمْ أَنَّهُ لَا إِلٰهَ إِلَّا اللَّهُ
وتالله وبالله والله

Testimonials: My heart is calm and not thinking of worldly matters.

Name: Khalilullah Bin Basri
Age: 17 years

بِسْمِ اللهِ الرَّحْمٰنِ الرَّحِيْمِ
اللَّهُمَّ صَلِّ عَلَى مُحَمَّدٍ وَعَلَى آلِ مُحَمَّدٍ

فَاعْلَمْ أَنَّهُ لَا إِلٰهَ إِلَّا اللَّهُ
وتالله وبالله والله

<u>Testimonials</u>: SubhanALLAH سبحانه و تعالى, ALLAH سبحانه و تعالى Almighty.

Alhamdulillah O ALLAH سبحانه و تعالى! You have given me Hidayah. O ALLAH سبحانه و تعالى! Bring me closer to you and to Muhammad ﷺ, Anbiya'-anbiya' سبحانه و تعالى, Sheikh ALLAH سبحانه و تعالى, ALLAH سبحانه و تعالى. Amin Ya ALLAH سبحانه و تعالى.

****

Name: Supriadi
Age: 60 years

بِسْمِ اللهِ الرَّحْمٰنِ الرَّحِيْمِ
اللَّهُمَّ صَلِّ عَلَى مُحَمَّدٍ وَعَلَى آلِ مُحَمَّدٍ
فَاعْلَمْ أَنَّهُ لَا إِلٰهَ إِلَّا اللَّهُ
وتالله وبالله والله

<u>Testimonials</u>: Alhamdulillah feel calm, thankful to have received the highest reward from the mercy of ALLAH سبحانه و تعالى.

Name: Kemalawati
Age: 53 years

بِسْمِ اللهِ الرَّحْمٰنِ الرَّحِيْمِ

اللَّهُمَّ صَلِّ عَلَى مُحَمَّدٍ وَعَلَى آلِ مُحَمَّدٍ

فَاعْلَمْ أَنَّهُ لَا إِلَهَ إِلَّا اللَّهُ

وتالله وبالله والله

Testimonials: When receiving the bai'at zikrul anfas, I cannot open my mouth, cannot open my eyes but my heart feels so happy. The time when istighfar was read. I feel like water was flowing through my veins. My body vibrated like "electric shock" and continued with syahadah with my hand raised up.

Right thumb entered my heart and wrote ALLAH سبحانه و تعالى's name. After that both thumbs wrote ALLAH سبحانه و تعالى's name right down to my feet.

When I close my eyes, I see in front of me a very long tunnel and in there is a clean blue colored water spinning, with white colored pebbles.

****

Name: Siti Khadijah (Aceh)
Age: 21 years

بِسْمِ اللهِ الرَّحْمٰنِ الرَّحِيْمِ
اللَّهُمَّ صَلِّ عَلَى مُحَمَّدٍ وَعَلَى آلِ مُحَمَّدٍ
فَاعْلَمْ أَنَّهُ لَا إِلٰهَ إِلَّا اللَّهُ
وتالله وبالله والله

Testimonials: When I closed my eyes, I saw 4 junctions and white light in front. I followed the white light. When I reached the junction, I saw my 2 children. I heard the sister asks the brother where he wanted to go. The brother answered, he wants to follow mother. Light that looks like the Sun.

****

Name: Mrs. Badarul Hisham
Age: 50

بِسْمِ اللهِ الرَّحْمٰنِ الرَّحِيْمِ
اللَّهُمَّ صَلِّ عَلَى مُحَمَّدٍ وَعَلَى آلِ مُحَمَّدٍ
فَاعْلَمْ أَنَّهُ لَا إِلٰهَ إِلَّا اللَّهُ
وتالله وبالله والله

Testimonials: Feel that I was inside the Ka'abah and there was a man in the Ka'abah. I ask to the man, who are you? Deep inside my heart says that it is Sheikh Dr Ismail.

Name: Mrs. Zalima
Age: 65 years

بِسْمِ اللهِ الرَّحْمٰنِ الرَّحِيْمِ
اللَّهُمَّ صَلِّ عَلَى مُحَمَّدٍ وَعَلَى آلِ مُحَمَّدٍ
فَاعْلَمْ أَنَّهُ لَا إِلٰهَ إِلَّا اللَّهُ
وتالله وبالله والله

Testimonials: Syukran to ALLAH سبحانه و تعالى, the feeling of peace cannot be described with words. Only tears can give the answer.

****

Name: Noraini Nordin
Age: xxx

بِسْمِ اللهِ الرَّحْمٰنِ الرَّحِيْمِ
اللَّهُمَّ صَلِّ عَلَى مُحَمَّدٍ وَعَلَى آلِ مُحَمَّدٍ
فَاعْلَمْ أَنَّهُ لَا إِلٰهَ إِلَّا اللَّهُ
وتالله وبالله والله

Testimonials: I see myself in a big field doing zikr and feeling very calm and contented. The light is very bright and I do not feel afraid at all.

****

Name: Asfia Sofwa Safuan

Age: 16 years

بِسْمِ اللهِ الرَّحْمٰنِ الرَّحِيْمِ
اللَّهُمَّ صَلِّ عَلَى مُحَمَّدٍ وَعَلَى آلِ مُحَمَّدٍ
فَاعْلَمْ أَنَّهُ لَا إِلٰهَ إِلَّا اللّٰهُ
وتالله وبالله والله

Testimonials: A sense of calm, sad and overwhelmed

****

Name: Nuramanina

Age: 17 years

بِسْمِ اللهِ الرَّحْمٰنِ الرَّحِيْمِ
اللَّهُمَّ صَلِّ عَلَى مُحَمَّدٍ وَعَلَى آلِ مُحَمَّدٍ
فَاعْلَمْ أَنَّهُ لَا إِلٰهَ إِلَّا اللّٰهُ
وتالله وبالله والله

Testimonials: Feels as if floating in another world

****

Name: Nur Arifah A'ala Mohd Yazid

Age: 13 years

بِسْمِ اللهِ الرَّحْمٰنِ الرَّحِيْمِ
اللَّهُمَّ صَلِّ عَلَى مُحَمَّدٍ وَعَلَى آلِ مُحَمَّدٍ

فَاعْلَمْ أَنَّهُ لَا إِلَهَ إِلَّا اللَّهُ

وتالله وبالله والله

Testimonials: A sense of calm, but feels sad when remembering my past sins...

****

Name: Siti khadidjah

Age: 57 years

بِسْمِ اللهِ الرَّحْمٰنِ الرَّحِيْمِ

اللَّهُمَّ صَلِّ عَلَى مُحَمَّدٍ وَعَلَى آلِ مُحَمَّدٍ

فَاعْلَمْ أَنَّهُ لَا إِلَهَ إِلَّا اللَّهُ

وتالله وبالله والله

Testimonials: I feel very happy, with more zikr, my body feels as though it's flying, as if I was in Medina.

****

From: Pakistan

Name: Muhammad Naseer Muhammad Bashir Gujar
Age: 33 Years
From: Narowal, Pakistan

بِسْمِ اللهِ الرَّحْمٰنِ الرَّحِيْمِ
اللَّهُمَّ صَلِّ عَلَى مُحَمَّدٍ وَعَلَى آلِ مُحَمَّدٍ

فَاعْلَمْ أَنَّهُ لَا إِلٰهَ إِلَّا اللَّهُ

وتالله وبالله والله

Testimonials: Heart kept feeling happy, and peaceful.
Problems which formerly gave me a headache, now
there is no such problem. Heart is doing zikr, my family
is already happy and pleased with me. Always miss
zikrullah, and the honorable Sheikh. Now I have no
problem dealing with heavy task, heart is always in
peace. My heart does not want dunia but more towards
"akhirat" or Afterlife.

****

Name: Omar Farouk
Age: 15 Years
From: Narowal, Pakistan

بِسْمِ اللهِ الرَّحْمٰنِ الرَّحِيْمِ

اللَّهُمَّ صَلِّ عَلٰى مُحَمَّدٍ وَعَلٰى آلِ مُحَمَّدٍ

فَاعْلَمْ أَنَّهُ لَا إِلٰهَ إِلَّا اللَّهُ

وتالله وبالله والله

Testimonials: My heart is more peaceful and happy.
Always misses the honourable Sheikh Dr Ismail Kassim
and longs for majlis ilmu and zikr.

****

Name: Muhammad Nawaz bin Muhammad Ashraf
Age: 35 Years
From: Narowal, Pakistan

بِسْمِ اللهِ الرَّحْمٰنِ الرَّحِيْمِ
اللَّهُمَّ صَلِّ عَلَى مُحَمَّدٍ وَعَلَى آلِ مُحَمَّدٍ
فَاعْلَمْ أَنَّهُ لَا إِلٰهَ إِلَّا اللَّهُ
وتالله وبالله والله

<u>Testimonials</u>: Prior to having Zikrul anfas, I always visit the Maqams or Tombs of Awliya ALLAH سبحانه و تعالى in Pakistan. I seek solace and peace. However, my heart is never at ease each time I visit a Maqam. My heart is still in disarray. I always have a black, angry or worried look on my face.

After getting Zikrul anfas, my heart is always calm, at ease, and very happy. My friends talked about my expression being different. Now I look more relaxed, radiant and always smiling. I feel so peaceful.

****

Name: Usman Khan
Age: 22 Years
From: Lahore, Pakistan

بِسْمِ اللهِ الرَّحْمٰنِ الرَّحِيْمِ
اللَّهُمَّ صَلِّ عَلَى مُحَمَّدٍ وَعَلَى آلِ مُحَمَّدٍ

فَاعْلَمْ أَنَّهُ لَا إِلٰهَ إِلَّا اللَّهُ

وتالله وبالله والله

<u>Testimonials</u>: I feel peaceful, relax and happy. If I don't do zikr, I feel sad.

****

Name: Malik Ifthikar

Age: 21 Years

From: Lahore, Pakistan

بِسْمِ اللهِ الرَّحْمٰنِ الرَّحِيْمِ

اللَّهُمَّ صَلِّ عَلَى مُحَمَّدٍ وَعَلَى آلِ مُحَمَّدٍ

فَاعْلَمْ أَنَّهُ لَا إِلٰهَ إِلَّا اللَّهُ

وتالله وبالله والله

<u>Testimonials</u>: Assalamualaikum, To all my friends and relatives, let me tell you a personal move or hijrah that changed my life, my thoughts, and my personal self.

My friends, I did not have good character-I did not do my Fajr prayer in a month. ALLAH hu Akbar. But one day, I met Sheikh Dr Ismail Kassim from Malaysia and he is my Pir, Sarkar. I first met him in Charkay Mosque. He was delivering the speech on the topic of Kalimah. He said you cannot get happiness without the Zikrul Anfas. If you do zikr with your heart, you will get peace and happiness in the hereafter. I was doing the zikr that day. I made zikrul anfas as the goal of my life. After doing the zikrul anfas, I felt peaceful and very happy. Now, after meeting Sheikh Dr Ismail Kassim, I pray 5 times a day, regularly.

I pray to ALLAH سبحانه و تعالى to give Sheikh a good reward, InsyaALLAH سبحانه و تعالى. I feel a lot better now compared to before receiving the zikr of breath. One day, I was doing my zikrul Anfas, with full focus and this course. I saw images in the moon. There were the images of Sheikh, and someone which I am not familiar with. My humble request to all the people of the world-Do the zikr Kalimah with heart, not tongue. If you do zikr, ALLAH سبحانه و تعالى will give you peace in this world and until judgement day ... ...
REGARD BY IFTIKHAR AWAN FROM PAKISTAN

****

Name: Ali Gujjar Khizar
Age: -undisclosed-
From: Islamabad, Pakistan

بِسْمِ اللهِ الرَّحْمٰنِ الرَّحِيْمِ
اللَّهُمَّ صَلِّ عَلَى مُحَمَّدٍ وَعَلَى آلِ مُحَمَّدٍ
فَاعْلَمْ أَنَّهُ لَا إِلٰهَ إِلَّا اللَّهُ
وتالله وبالله والله

Testimonials: I remember during the time when I was talqin with zikrul anfas by our mursyid, Sheikh Ismail Kassim, I saw the word of 'ALLAH سبحانه و تعالى'.

Now, I feel very peaceful in my life. I feel that ALLAH سبحانه و تعالى is always there with me. Alhamdulillah.

****

Name: Qari Abdul Wahid
Age: -undisclosed-
From: Lahore, Pakistan
<u>Testimonials</u>:

بِسْمِ اللهِ الرَّحْمٰنِ الرَّحِيْمِ
اللَّهُمَّ صَلِّ عَلَى مُحَمَّدٍ وَعَلَى آلِ مُحَمَّدٍ
فَاعْلَمْ أَنَّهُ لَا إِلَهَ إِلَّا اللَّهُ
وتالله وبالله والله

Alhamdulillah after getting zikrul anfas from our mursyid, Sheikh Ismail Kassim, I feel tranquil and peaceful. Sometimes I can see the Kaaba when doing zikr anfas.

I remember during talqin zikrul anfas, I saw the nur of Rasullullah ﷺ and I cry when this happen.

There are also times when I dreamed of Rasullullah ﷺ during sleep.

I feel very close to Him now. Alhamdulillah.

****

Printed in the United States
By Bookmasters